T0198651

Why We Love Them So

Why We Love Them So

SURVIVING THE LOSS OF AN ANIMAL FRIEND

Father Paul A. Keenan

for The Perseus Foundation

WHY WE LOVE THEM SO

iUniverse books may be ordered through booksellers or by contacting:

iUniverse
1663 Liberty Drive
Bloomington, IN 47403
www.iuniverse.com
1-800-Authors (1-800-288-4677)

Because of the dynamic nature of the Internet, any web addresses or links contained in this book may have changed since publication and may no longer be valid. The views expressed in this work are solely those of the author and do not necessarily reflect the views of the publisher, and the publisher hereby disclaims any responsibility for them.

Any people depicted in stock imagery provided by Getty Images are models, and such images are being used for illustrative purposes only.
Certain stock imagery © Getty Images.

ISBN: 978-1-4401-4340-3 (sc)
ISBN: 978-1-4401-4338-0 (hc)
ISBN: 978-1-4401-4339-7 (e)

Library of Congress Control Number: 2009932559

Print information available on the last page.

iUniverse rev. date: 01/11/2019

Also by Father Paul Keenan

Good News for Bad Days:
Living a Soulful Life

St. Patrick

Stages of the Soul:
The Path of the Soulful Life

Heartstorming:
The Way to a Purposeful Life

Elisha's Jars: Enjoying Abundance & Prosperity
When Life Seems Limited

Beyond Blue Snow: Essays Toward the
Refreshment of the Soul

If You Want to Change Your Mind,
You Have to Open Your Heart

Praise for Father Paul Keenan's work
and
Why We Love Them So:
Surviving the Loss of an Animal Friend

"Father Keenan writes with compassion and with insight into the human-animal bond. Reading him, especially in regards to the need for wonder in our lives, I felt as if I were reading something of my own. This book should be of great help to those grieving over the loss of a beloved companion animal."

—Dean Koontz, author of *Odd Hours*

"*Why We Love Them So* gives us comfort and understanding while guiding us through our profound grief over the loss of a pet. While sharing his own struggles and challenges with grieving his pets, Father Paul offers us heartfelt suggestions and a highly-enlightened perspective. Anyone who has ever gone through the loss of a pet will greatly appreciate this book. *Why We Love Them So* is a lasting testament of Father Paul's enduring love for animals."

—June Cotner, author of *Animal Blessings* and *Dog Blessings*

"*Why We Love Them So* is a wonderful commentary on our deepest relationships with our pets."

—James Redfield, author of *The Celestine Prophecy*

"A touching book that reminds me to cherish every moment with my pets."

—Salle Merrill Redfield, author of *Creating a Life of Joy*

"Uplifting, sage advice from one of America's foremost spiritual teachers."

—Wayne W. Dyer, author of *Your Sacred Self*

"A guide for finding inner peace in a fast-paced world."

—Richard Carlson, author of *Don't Sweat the Small Stuff*

"Brings the practice of spirituality to a very practical level."

—Deepak Chopra, author of *The Seven Spiritual Laws of Success*

"Down-to-earth and full of wisdom. I didn't sense a wrong note anywhere—an achievement in a book about the soul's mysterious ways."

—Thomas Moore, author of *Care of the Soul*

"With tremendous insight, compassion, and understanding of the human heart, Father Keenan has written a modern classic about abundance and the gifts available to us all."

—Luanne Rice, author of *Summer of Roses*

"Keenan accomplishes the feat of discussing the realities of everyday life from a genuinely spiritual point of view ... [and] guides readers to rediscover the sacred in the ordinary."

—*Publishers Weekly*

"Gentle wisdom, humor, and plain good sense.... Keenan's language is memorable in its earthiness and simplicity ... a pure pleasure to read."

—*Southern Pines Pilot* (NC)

"Teddy's book"

in memory of

Pan Gu Brown,

who lost his courageous battle with cancer

on September 30, 2008.

He went to Heaven and to Father Paul.

"Sometimes he will sit upon the carpet in front of you with eyes so melting, so caressing and human, that they almost frighten you, for it is impossible to believe that a soul is not there."

Theophile Gaulier (1811–72)

All proceeds from this book go to The Perseus Foundation,
to fund cancer research
to benefit our canine and feline friends
and The Magic Bullet Fund;
establish Father Paul's Thaddeus Bear Fund
for kitties needing care for cancer, FIP, or other illnesses;
and launch Father Paul's beloved Pets and Pals Project
in Washington, D.C.,
bringing together children who have cancer and
dogs who have survived cancer.

cover photo: *SPIKE & YOUNG PAUL*

Acknowledgments

It is with profound gratitude that I thank Victoria Brown and The Perseus Foundation for making the publication of this book possible. She willingly and courageously forged ahead with Father Paul's final book after his untimely and sudden death on June 10, 2008, three days before he would have turned sixty-two.

How do we thank Father Paul for his wise counsel and loving consolation, soulfulness, and friendship that he so generously bestowed upon us in his all-too-short life? He penned this completed book (including title page, table of contents, foreword, and A Final Note), gave it to The Perseus Foundation, and made one set of changes as they appear here before his passing. We have added only publication details of endorsements, copyright, dedication and quotation, blessing prayer, directory of resources, as well as photographs from Father Paul's personal collection, and these acknowledgments. I am privileged to team with Victoria and Perseus to bring Father Paul's "Stages of the Grieving Soul" and "Soulful Musings" to fruition.

Bless all of you who grieve, those who care for the grieving, those who love and care for our earth's animals, those who love and pray for Father Paul, as well as those who donate to The Perseus Foundation.

Could we ever thank our furry friends enough for their love and presence in our lives? They inspired this book. Among them are Dear and Princess, Teddy J Bear and Flicka Anne/Lilla, Lionel Franklin (named after two radio hosts) and Sherman, Katheryne "Kitty" Taylor, Tabitha Lynne, Chesie, Muffin, Spike and Bounce, Peter, Pan Gu and Perseus Brown.

I am thankful to Father Paul's friends who encouraged and supported me through his final projects: Vince Gardino, Frank Ruta, Bob and Patrice Martin, Lisa Franks, Sister Lyn Sparling, Christine Brush, Joe and Mary Barletti, Pam Detrow, Linda Giordano, Sharron Charlton and Father Bartholomew Daly, and Reverend Laurie Sue Brockway and Reverend Victor Fuhrman.

Thank you to Hortense Baffa, Jane Hurley, Irene Farrelly, Margaret Andrews and Vivien Scofield who support me through everything and, my sister, Chris McConnell, who has been there for me in so many ways, especially, since Father Paul's passing.

Thank you also to Sarah Molinari who preserved Father Paul's articles for his Web site, Stephen Garrett who archived Father Paul's writings, and Dilcia Gonzalez who takes such loving care of me, all of whom helped me submit this book for publication.

Thank you to everyone who listened to my stories for hours on end, you know who you are, viewed photos and helped me make the myriad of decisions this past year.

I am grateful to Eulala and Allan Conner for their artistic touch. Last but, certainly, not least is June Cotner, "Aunt" to Father Paul's first book and Fairy Godmother to me, generously sharing her resources for his final book. Credit is due as well to Sarah Disbrow of iUniverse for assisting us neophytes, especially, in our author's absence, and to the editors there, who praised Father Paul's writing with each read. Without all these people, this book could never have reached you, dear readers, and certainly not as it appears here.

Thank you so much to Dr. Kristopher Hansen for his life-saving surgery of Father Paul's beloved kitty, Dear, on March 12, 2009.

Annuit Coeptis

Susan Zappo
Father Paul's friend
November 19, 2008

Happy Anniversaries (Ordination June 3, Death June 10)

and Birthday (June 13) in Heaven, Paul

With heartfelt gratitude to Pan Gu's doctors: Dr. Chand Khanna and his phenomenal team at Friendship Hospital for Animals, Washington, D.C. You are truly outstanding. Dr. Nancy Gustafson and her compassionate team at The Regional Veterinary Referral Center, Springfield, VA. You gave it your best shot, and we thank you ever so much. Dr. Elsa Beck at The Hope Center for Advanced Veterinary Medicine, Vienna, VA. Your diagnosis, experience, and knowledge were invaluable. With deep gratitude to all veterinary oncologists who care for our pets with cancer. The Perseus Foundation stands tall and proud behind you. Together we are making a difference. Simona, your love for Pan Gu shined brightly during those long nights that you comforted and watched over "a boy named Gu."

And for Ernesto Brown: Pan Gu considered you his human! Your devotion to this mischief maker, your incredible generosity, and Pan Gu's love for you were as unique as they were precious to behold. You, too, are one of a kind.

Victoria Brown
Pan Gu's second favorite human
and Perseus Magic's most favorite human
December 3, 2008

Contents

Foreword

Since you are reading this book, you have probably lost a pet and are feeling very sad. Having lost many pets over the years in various ways, I know that while I can never hope to understand exactly what you are feeling, in a way, I do understand. I especially want to say to you that what you are feeling right now is very normal and very right. Grieving the loss of our pets is an important way of honoring their place in our lives. We mourn because we loved them and they loved us, and that love is irreplaceable. Please don't let anyone tell you that it is not right to grieve or that you should get over it because it's "only" an animal. People say the most foolish things sometimes because they don't really know what to say. Take your time. Grieve. Let yourself be sad. It's perfectly reasonable.

Yet since you are reading this book, I want to leave you in a better place at the end than you were when you picked up this book. I don't want you to stay sad. I want you to see that what feels like a very negative experience right now can make a very positive contribution to your life. The problem with most of our grieving, including when we mourn our animals, is that we've never been taught what to do with our grief. It seems like such a block to what we want to do in life and where we want to go. It seems like something that paralyzes us. Yet if we are patient with ourselves, if we take the time and the effort to understand our grief, we will gradually find ourselves able to grasp its power to transform us. Grieving can help us to understand our lives in a profound way, and can actually enable us to face the future more confidently and successfully. I can promise you that you will always mourn the pets you have lost, but I can also promise you that your grief can transform your life.

As I write this, I am just a little over two weeks from the loss of my twenty-five-year-old cat, Teddy, and, as you might expect, I have been giving a great deal of thought to the grieving process. I have been concerned about my own grieving, about the grieving of friends who knew Teddy well, and about how Dear, my seven-year-old cat, grieves the loss of her friend.

My one great impression of these days since Teddy died is that my space is too quiet and life is somehow off-center. When he was in his prime, Teddy used to romp and play with Dear. Dear would chase Teddy all around, and it seemed to me that Teddy (brains were not his strong suit) harbored the belief that if you were first in the race that meant you won. It never dawned on him that the cat chasing him from behind was the winner. Dear loved to play hockey with little plastic balls with bells in them, and she would romp for hours while Teddy slept. Then there was Teddy's "voice," demanding food, grieving in his morning ritual for his long-time companion Flicka, or pontificating from the windowsill or bathroom sink. When Teddy was around, there was plenty of noise and activity. Now, it is very quiet, and that is different.

I find myself missing every aspect of my routines with Teddy over the eighteen years we were together. I miss his demands for food. I miss his curling up in my lap to go to sleep. I miss picking him up at the end when he couldn't make the jump himself. Life is, yes, just off-center without him. Something is definitely missing, and it's uncomfortable.

Is there any way of mapping how we can deal with grief? Everyone's grief is different, yet is there a way in which we can come to terms with what is going on and what we can expect? Let's be clear: the soul makes its own rules and steadfastly refuses to follow ours, yet can we discover the ways of the soul so as to understand what is happening when we grieve, and what we might expect to happen next?

Far and away, the greater part of the literature on grieving harkens back to the stages of grief proposed by Elisabeth Kübler-Ross in her *On Death and Dying.* Those stages are: denial, anger, depression, bargaining, and acceptance. Most people know those stages like the back of their hand, and they certainly do make an excellent map for understanding the lay of the grieving process.

Yet sometimes it helps to look at the same phenomena through different lenses, and I think that is true for how we grieve when we lose our animal companions. In 1999, I wrote a book called *Stages of the Soul: The Path of the Soulful Life* (Contemporary Books) in which I denoted seven stages through which the soul makes the journey from being a lost soul to being re-enchanted with everyday life. All of us who reflect upon the experiences of our lives at some point or other refer to ourselves or to others as "lost souls." Is it possible for us to make the journey through to a meaningful and purposeful life? In that book, I argue that it is; and through examples and stories, I set out to show that if we listen to our soul, it can move us through seven stages of development which, in the end, leave our hearts singing again. The basic prerequisite is that we turn within and listen. Once we do that, and if we do that consistently, the soul can do the rest.

Here I would like to propose that these same seven stages of the soul can help us to map our stages of grief when we lose an animal friend. What I prefer about this approach is that it consistently takes us back to the soul, which is the deepest and most precious part of us—the part where we encounter God—and invites us to stay in touch with the deepest recesses of ourselves. I cannot stress sufficiently the point that going through grief—whether for a human or for an animal—is not simply a matter of passing from stage to stage until healing takes place. Rather it is a matter of learning to open our personal resources to a life that is spiritually rich and inspired. In my book *Good News for Bad Days: Living Soulful Life* (Warner Books, 1998), I proposed the idea that the so-called worst days of our lives can turn out to be the best things that ever happened to us, and that we have within us a soul that is able to make sense of what, to our ordinary sensory and mental categories, is unreasonable and senseless. The soul is the weaver that ties the threads of our experiences together and makes them into something that conveys depth and meaning. If we allow it to weave us, we will discover patterns of living that far outshine anything that we can accomplish through our own independent initiatives.

As we begin to explore this possibility, it is important for us to understand that grieving and healing are not just things that superficially happen to us and that can be "dealt with" by some sort of system or other. Grieving and healing are profound experiences of the soul and as such can lead us, if we let them, to an entirely higher way of living. I am not proposing here a method for getting us "back to normal" after the loss of an animal. I am, rather, proposing a way of understanding our grieving and healing that will allow us to open ourselves to the possibility of an entirely different way of living. If anything, we will be getting ourselves to the non-normal, since we'll be operating at levels of being and awareness that far transcend the fix-it attitude that permeates so much of healing work today. It is as if we will be saying to our departed animal friends (*à la* Elizabeth Barrett Browning), "How do I love thee? Let me count the ways. / I love thee with the depth and breadth and height / My soul can reach, When feeling out of sight / For the ends of Being and Ideal Grace."

We must make a choice. Either we go through our grieving with an eye to fixing ourselves and getting back to normal, or we do our grieving with an eye to opening ourselves to a life of Being and Ideal Grace. It is the latter course that I propose here.

What, then, are the stages of the soul? They are, first, the "Lost Soul," the feeling of numbness and aloneness after death, my feeling that my life is too quiet and off-center after the death of Teddy. Then there is the stage that I call "Falling Through the Cracks," where my grief takes a "Why me?" or "Why only me?" sort of turn. The third stage is "Compassion," as we realize that losses such as these are experienced by others who can help us and whom, in turn, we can help. Then there is the stage called "Tapestry," when we become aware of the patterns in our losses and our healings that can reveal to us something of a sense of overall purpose in our lives. I call the fifth stage "Attic Wisdom," because it is very much as though the soul takes us up into the attic and allows us to sort through the stored-up experiences of our lives and make hay of them. Sixth, there is the inevitable "Return" to daily life. We cannot stay in the attic forever; we have work to do at home. Finally, there is the stage called "Re-enchantment," where we find ourselves committed to the new level of aliveness and of reality that is the essence of the soulful life.

Let us, then, explore these stages of the soul. Let us open ourselves to the possibility that we can do more than get on with life, and that our animal companions can allow us, in death as in life, to grow to the life of beauty and ideal grace that is our birthright.

This book will take us through the stages of the soul as we mourn the loss of our beloved animal companion. It will also provide a section of short reflections on various aspects of grieving. It does not have to be read in any particular order. Let your soul guide you as to what to read next. Like grieving itself, reading this book is meant to be an adventure, with all of the spontaneity a true adventure requires.

Part One:
The Stages of the Grieving Soul

Stage One: Lost Soul

In dealing with the life of the soul, one cardinal principle is that things are not always—or often—what they seem to be. In our ordinary experience, people pretty much tend to take things at face value. What is, is; and what is, is what appears to be.

That doesn't work for the soul. The soul always takes a higher perspective, and from that higher perspective it sees things much differently from the way we see them in our ordinary way of considering things. That is why I was able to say earlier that some of our worst days have been some of the best things that ever happened to us. At the time, we don't see it; it's only when we have had some time to get a better perspective on things that we see the blessings and the gifts that came with the grief.

We especially need to keep this in mind with this first stage of grief, which I call "Lost Soul." What we experience at this stage is profound disorientation and tragedy, and it seems that no good will ever come from it. While we need to honor this experience and to let it be, we also need to have in the back of our minds the realization that this is not the end of the story by any means. The experience of loss leaves us feeling disoriented, and it is a good idea for us to allow each side of the equation to play itself out.

When we've lost an animal companion, our first feeling is that we ourselves are lost. Earlier, I mentioned that in the aftermath of Teddy's death, I am feeling that life is a bit off-center. That's a fairly common feeling when we have lost a beloved pet. One night a friend went home, fed her eighteen-month-old kitten, moments later heard him scream, and watched him collapse in death. It was a heart attack. She remembers sitting with the dead kitty in her arms, staring in disbelief that this kitten, who moments ago had been so lively, was now dead in her arms. We often call this stage "denial," but I think there is much more to it than that. Denial is part of it—we're shocked and taken aback by what we see. But there is more to it than that. The loss, whether sudden or prolonged, leaves us feeling lost, as though we are in unfamiliar territory and don't know what to do.

I remember experiencing this feeling for a month when I was in a rectory on the Lower East Side of Manhattan and one of our kittens, a beautiful black and white longhair whom I had named Muffin, went missing. It was particularly frightening because there were feral cats around and she was a timid soul who would never survive such danger. Like many of our cats, Muffin had come to us as a stray, and I especially loved her gentle spirit. Day after long day for an entire month, I would go downstairs hoping to find her, and every day realized anew that she was gone. At the time, there was a popular song, "She's Gone," and those words echoed from the pit of my stomach. I still had Teddy and Flicka upstairs, but Muffin was gone.

Muffin's story ended well. A lady in the parish kindly posted pictures of Muffin on the lampposts, and someone found her and brought her back. But it was a long month without her, I can tell you. One of the pillars of my existence had been pulled out from under me, and I felt it deeply.

I had had a similar feeling earlier when I was five years old, and my uncle decided it was time for me to have a dog. So he brought in Bounce, a black and white fox terrier puppy, who was entirely wrong for me and for our household. Lesson: be very careful about selecting a dog for a child. Bounce was extremely nervous and skittish and not at all bright. He never mastered the art of potty training and was a constant nuisance to my parents. He was also a worry: if I went to play with him or got too close to his food, he would bite me. My parents finally had enough. One morning I woke up, looked for Bounce, but he was gone. My parents refused to tell me what had happened to him. So there I was, five years old, my dog was gone, and nobody would tell me what had happened. Talk about feeling lost. To this day, I do not know what happened to Bounce, but I can only assume that they had him euthanized. I got over feeling lost, of course, but traces of that feeling over Bounce remain with me today. It was really a disorienting experience.

I use the examples of Muffin and Bounce to illustrate the fact that losses of pets can and do come in other ways besides death. Regardless, the grieving is the same and it is intense.

I have said that in these stages of the soul, our soul guides us toward a knowledge and understanding that is beyond what we are getting from our intellect and our senses. What is it that we can learn from this stage of feeling lost?

The first lesson to be learned when we feel like lost souls is that although we feel lost, we are not really as lost as we feel. One of the key principles in dealing with any work of the soul is that there is a huge difference between reality and appearances. Our tendency is to fight and argue for the appearances—we know that we feel sad, even discouraged and depressed, and we are afraid that there is no way out. People may try to tell us that we "shouldn't" be sad or that we should "snap out of it," but sad is how we feel. That for us is our reality.

Though we need to acknowledge our sadness, a soulful approach to our loss demands that we keep, at least, in the back of our minds the idea that our sadness and sense of aloneness are not the end of the story. The soul's story is that, instead of being alone, we are part of a vast network of spirit by virtue of which we are in touch with every other soul. Though we feel lost, we nonetheless have a definite place in the overall scheme of things.

Especially after the deaths of Lionel (a wonderful older cat who was with me for eighteen months) and Teddy, I became aware of a vast network of people who had suffered similar losses and who hastened to express through cards, e-mails, and phone calls their profound understanding of what I was going through. I felt alone and isolated, but thanks to those wonderful friends I was able to keep alive the sense that I was not as alone as I felt. I was somehow able to feel less isolated, more normal, in my grieving.

A second realization that comes with a soulful approach to our feeling like a lost soul is that our sense of feeling lost is not an endpoint (as it seems) but rather is a step into the realm of mystery. All too often today, we are encouraged to treat the circumstances of life as problems, indeed, as one problem after another. It is of the essence of a problem that it is there to be fixed. When we're feeling like lost souls, we are tempted to do things that will assuage our grief. Sometimes we take to alcohol or drugs, or overindulgence in food or entertainment. The problem is, grief will not abate unless we stop trying to fix it and instead let it lead us into a sense of the mystery of things. The loss of a pet is not a problem to be resolved; it is an entry into the mystery of life and death. Living soulfully instead of at the level of "fixes," we learn to allow the mystery of our grieving to wash over us, to teach us, to give us some perspective on the depth of life.

Concurrent with this is the often-forgotten fact that the dark experiences of life are also part of life, and if we let them, they can gift us with a tenderness of heart that will take us a long way in our dealings with our own life and with the lives of others. The implementation of this insight can be very practical. After Teddy's death, it was tempting for me to remove his blankets on which he died, the futon and doggie steps that I had bought for him, and put them away. I realized that if I did that, it would be tantamount to denying that Teddy ever existed. I realized that I didn't want to make the house look as though Teddy had never been here. I held off washing his blanket on the sofa, because I knew that I still had his smell, and I noticed that Dear loved to cuddle up in it, presumably for that reason. I found a lot of strength in keeping these "sacred places" of Teddy's life.

One of the reasons that feeling like a lost soul often seems so awful and so terrifying is that we are just beginning to learn (or relearn) the language of the soul. It may seem strange to think of the soul as having a language, but it does and we can learn to understand it. It's not usually a language like the human voice. Rather, it's a much more subtle and intuitive sort of thing, more or less what Pascal speaks of when he alludes to "the reasons of the heart." In her best-selling novel, *Silver Bells* (Bantam Books, 2004), Luanne Rice tells the story of Catherine, a young widow deeply grieving the loss of her husband. When she is looking for advice as to how to help a troubled young man in the story, Catherine goes to her church to pray. There, she encounters the spirit of her late husband, whose advice she asks. His reply is one of the best descriptions I have seen of the language of the soul: "I cannot tell you what to do, but I can show you."

That's the way of the soul. The soul works by innuendo, by seeming coincidence, by internal suggestion or intuition, guiding us and leading us as we journey. When we are lost souls, we are really not so lost—we are in the beginning stages of learning to go inward for advice, to notice the seeming coincidences that take place. When Flicka died, followed by the sudden death of a dear friend, I went inside and listened to the intuition that it was time to bring another kitty home. Miraculously, the Humane Society stayed open past closing time for me, and, sure enough, there, waiting for me, was the beautiful little kitten that I now call Dear. My soul, though not telling me what to do, was showing me what to do. In the early stages of our grieving, we can remind ourselves to look for that suggestive, coincidental, and intuitive guidance. Before long, we will be accustomed to drawing upon the advice of the soul.

Another learning from this "Lost Soul" stage on this journey of life is that we are here to learn (or some would say, to remember) the eternal truths of the universe. One of these truths is that things are not always what they seem. Another is that *being* is more important than *having* or *doing*. You know that as an "animal parent" —the time you spend just being with your animal friends is precious. You need to care for them, feed them, and so forth; but it's not the *doing* that makes the relationship; it's the *being*. Eternal truths like these, once impressed upon our minds, change the pace at which we live and the way in which we live. Knowing that can help us to be patient with ourselves as we grieve, so that we do not tire ourselves with endless distractions.

A fifth learning from the stage of being a "Lost Soul" is that it is all right not to have immediate answers to everything. Sometimes we just have to ask for guidance and allow ourselves to free-float. Not quite knowing what to do does not mean that we're stupid or incompetent. It means we're learning, and that's what life is really all about.

Finally, in this "Lost Soul" stage, we can learn that part of the allure of the soulful life is that it is neither entirely absent from us nor fully consciously present. Even if we are beginners, we can lead a soulful life, or what Wayne Dyer in his book *Inspiration* (Hay House, 2006) calls "an inspired life." Leading a soulful life can and often does take place when our hearts are broken; and, as we have seen, these dark and painful times can teach us many important truths. There is a gift in them. Often, when we think in terms of "successful living," we are given the impression that it is something that comes at the end of a long process. Soulful living is not like that. It is something we can experience here and now, even though we will continue (hopefully) to grow in inspiration as the years go on.

The stage of being a "Lost Soul" is an important stage in our healing and in our growth in soulfulness. We may feel as though we are going nowhere, just spinning our wheels in the mire of grief, but if we learn to pay attention to our soul (and not allow ourselves to be trapped in the limitations of what we are experiencing), we find that we are getting somewhere, learning something new about how to evaluate our experiences and how to live.

BABY DEAR & DADDY PAUL, 2000

DEAR IN A BOX

Stage Two: Falling Through the Cracks

As we go through the soulful stages of grief, we are learning that we cannot always trust in appearances. I say this here because, as we consider this second stage of grief, it may appear to us that things are getting worse rather than getting better. It may feel that way, but take heart: the soul is at work deep within you, and there is nothing to be afraid of. Before long, you will find yourself on solid ground.

The stage that I call "Falling Through the Cracks" represents that feeling we can have that all of the bad luck in the universe is coming in our direction, or at least a disproportionate share of it. We wonder why others seem to get off so lightly while every bad thing conceivable seems to come our way.

I call this stage "Falling Through the Cracks" because its dynamics remind me of a remark made by a volunteer youth catechist in a parish I worked in years ago. She said that she enjoyed working with economically poor kids because without someone to watch out for them, they could easily fall through the cracks. It was true. In the absence of someone to notice them, certain kids would go off by themselves and get into terrible trouble. This woman remarked that something like this had happened to her when she was a teenager. Had it not been for a kindly nun, she would never have finished high school but would have dropped out and gone unnoticed.

When we are experiencing loss or some other sorrow, it can often seem to us that we are falling through the cracks. Other people seem to have guardian angels that watch out for them, but ours seems to have gone on vacation. Other people seem to be blessed; we seem to draw anything but blessings. I mentioned earlier that when Flicka died, the very next day a good friend dropped dead of a heart attack. A few months prior to that, one of my devoted listeners and friends passed away, and the day after his funeral, we lost John Cardinal O'Connor, Archbishop of New York, with whom I had enjoyed a warm relationship. By the end of that summer, I wondered if I would ever do anything again but say good-bye to people I loved. I felt like I had fallen though the cracks.

Of course, things are not as cut and dried as they seem, and grief can diminish our ability to recognize that. Others are going through their private hells, too; it's just that we're going through ours, and it's hard for us to see anyone else's. Also, since others are going through their own hard times, they, in turn, might not take the time to notice us going through ours. So we feel not only lost, but isolated and alone.

What are the things we feel when going through the stage of "Falling Through the Cracks"? For one thing, we feel as though there is no solid ground for us to stand on. We literally feel as though we are reeling, floating, free-falling. I remember when I was a boy, one afternoon the elderly lady who lived next door (with her married daughter and son-in-law) accidentally dropped a jar of peanut butter, which landed on the head of their beloved parakeet and killed it. I recall that for days and weeks, the entire family was absolutely distraught, most of all, of course, the mother, who could not stop blaming herself for their bird's death. As a kid, I thought it was all a bit ridiculous; but at that time, I had not had much experience with pets. Today, I can well understand the depth of their grief. When their bird died, their whole world fell apart; home wasn't home and life wasn't life anymore. That's what it feels like when you are falling through the cracks.

A second characteristic of this stage (and as you'll see it is related to the first) is that we keep looking outside of ourselves in the hope that something out there will stop our falling. We feel as though we'd do just about anything to fill up that awful gap. But the fact is, nothing that we try manages to eradicate the awful feeling that life has it in for us and for some reason is excluding us from its beneficence. This makes us feel, in turn, that the world is an unfriendly place, and that it is particularly unfriendly to us. We may read all sorts of self-help and inspirational books and articles, but our basic feeling at this point is that none of the things they say or recommend apply to us. The world has it in for us, and we are simply victims of unsolicited bad luck. Or, we might feel that some or even most of our bad luck is deserved. Perhaps we feel we are being punished, that God or life is taking it out on us for evil things we have done in the past. Perhaps we feel tremendous guilt over something we have done (or, for that matter, simply because significant people in our lives have told us that we are worthless or downright evil).

At this stage of "Falling Through the Cracks," there is a terrible feeling of aloneness. You feel singled out for disaster after disaster, and you feel, too, that there is no way out for you. You are condemned forever to fall through the cracks.

As horrible and painful as this stage is, it nonetheless is a legitimate stage of grieving, and moreover, it does not escape the influence of the soul. In fact, if we can allow ourselves to get quiet and to listen, we can hear the soul contradicting each and every one of the above impressions we have about life.

The first correction lies within the very nature of the soul itself. When falling through the cracks, we feel that there is no solid ground on which to land. The soul tells us that we do, indeed, have something solid and tangible on which to rely—namely the soul itself. When I was getting ready to go to college, my parents decided—without consulting me—to give away Spike, our beloved Boston terrier. My dad found a good home for him, and before long, Spike was gone. I don't think I had ever before felt so bereft. I longed to hold Spike and play with him. I could almost hear his paws on the hardwood floor and see him coming around the corner. It was awful. Already having jitters about going to college and about moving to a new house, having to give up Spike was just about the end and especially since I had no say in the matter. It was a done deal. Then, I was devastated, knowing nothing about the soul as a place of refuge. Today, in similar circumstances, I know that I can turn within. I won't necessarily feel better right away—unlike "fixes," soul work does not depend upon immediate results. But I know that there is a peaceful place within where I can put a stop to the sensation that I am falling into deeper and deeper misfortune. When I feel that I have no place to turn, my soul calls me home.

When we're tempted to turn outward to "fix" our feeling of falling through the cracks, the soul reminds us to turn inward. Even in the midst of pain, there is a satisfaction in knowing that we have this touchstone within us to turn to, a satisfaction that contradicts the ongoing disappointment we feel when we try remedy after remedy and find no lasting relief. In contrast to the feeling that happiness seems elusive and difficult to attain, the soul shows us that, as we accustom ourselves to making our home in it, life develops an unprecedented ease and effortlessness. Note that the reason for this ease and effortlessness is that we are allowing the soul's superior knowledge to guide us and to draw our greater good to us. For example, that's how I was guided to go to the Humane Society and find Dear after Flicka died. I let myself be guided, I made a phone call, they kept the office open for me past business hours, I went there, and there she was. When we're all tied up in knots, we naturally waver between paralysis and frenzied efforts to resolve our pain. The soul tells us that if we make it our home, ease and effortlessness become the order of the day. No longer do we feel that life has it in for us. Rather, we begin to feel that life has treasures to bestow upon us. It's quite a difference. As a result, the world no longer seems unfriendly and hostile to us, and after a while, we may even begin to feel that life is so good to us that it bestows upon us a purpose and a sense of well-being. There are still problems, yes; but now we know where to go with them.

The stage of "Falling Through the Cracks" really gets us through the worst part of the grieving process. Now that we have found in the soul a place to stand upon in our distress, the really good gifts that the soul can give us in our difficult time can begin to manifest. From the vantage point of the soul, life is better than it appears.

DEAR PEEKING

Stage Three: Compassion

I often think of the night I was coming back into New York City on a fairly late commuter train. The train was crowded, and I ended up sitting next to a young woman, who, as it turned out, had two cute little white fluff-ball doggies in her lap, Roxie and Trixie. One of the doggies started to snuggle up to me, and the woman and I started a conversation about our pets. It turned out that she was a lawyer who, because she didn't like practicing law, had begun doing volunteer work on behalf of animals. We swapped animal stories, and at one point in the conversation, the woman asked a rhetorical question I'll never forget: "Where, along the way, did we make the turn into insanity?" I knew right away that she was referring to the unique craziness that is the hallmark of true animal lovers. There's no doubt about it—we're a little mad. I remember my grandmother, Nana, who insisted that one day, after she had returned from a trip, her parakeet looked her in the eye and said, "Where the heck have you been?" Yes, we're crazy, but deep down we're all right. It's because we're crazy for our pets that we hurt so much when they leave us.

With the stages of the "Lost Soul" and "Falling Through the Cracks," we have made it through the most consistently painful parts of our grief journey. I must admit that, writing about it, it's hard not to make it sound as easy as 1-2-3. It's not easy at all, but once we know what's going on in the respective stages of our grief, it can be immensely rewarding. One thing about soul work, by the way, is that it doesn't happen within a particular time frame or schedule. Certainly, there are things we can do to move the process along, especially if we feel we have been stuck in a particular stage for a very long time. But everyone takes a different length of time to grieve, and for some people certain stages may be longer than for others. In some sense, we never stop mourning the pets we have lost. I still feel sad for Peter, the canary who went toes-up when I was three. But his loss doesn't paralyze me now because I have learned to put things into a larger perspective, and I have learned that there are things I can do (such as writing this book) that help me do something to help others and to use my grief in that way. A soulful process of grieving implies that we be patient with ourselves and allow ourselves to grieve in our own way.

One of the results of discovering that we have, after all, a soul to turn to (and that we are not as lost or as unlucky as we feel) is that we are led to understand that far from being alone, we share the experience of pet loss with others who are as "crazy" as we are about their pets and mourn them just as deeply as we mourn ours. This is where we take the turn into "Compassion," the third stage of the grieving soul. "Compassion" literally means "feeling with." Here, we learn to feel with others who are in similar circumstances to ours, and we deepen our sense of patience and understanding with ourselves.

I love the longshoreman philosopher Eric Hoffer's definition of compassion. He said, "Compassion is the antitoxin of the soul." When we are able to break through our own suffering and enter into awareness and understanding of the sufferings of others, then we are able to release much of the negative energy that has built up within us and that manifests in the happenings around us. Inner peace is at the heart of everything we want in life, but what blocks that inner peace is all of the negative energy that has built up because of our unhappy experiences and because of what others have taught us about life. As Hoffer says, such a situation is toxic. When we think of toxins, we normally think of poisons that have accumulated in our body. It may be a new revelation to say that there are spiritual toxins as well. Sadness, depression, anger, hatred, and the like are negative energies that poison the spirit within us. Now that we have developed the understanding that we are not alone in our grief and that, indeed, we do have somewhere to turn in the midst of it, we begin to feel safe. The walls of grief and despair begin to crumble, and we start to see that the inner peace we want is possible for us. We may not experience it in large doses yet, but at least we know that we are not excluded from its happening in us. Moreover, now that we realize that we are not alone in our suffering, we begin to take to heart the fact that others are suffering as well. This opens the door to compassion, as we realize that the peace and happiness we desire for ourselves are the peace and happiness that others desire for themselves. This, in turn, opens us more fully to our inner guidance as to what, if anything, we can do for ourselves and for others in pain. Compassion softens our hearts as it drains them of their toxicity. It literally transforms us into new people. I would not dream today of harboring the feelings I had years ago when my neighbors lost their bird. My experiences with caring for and losing animals have helped me to grow in understanding and compassion. I am not, I am happy to say, the person I was back then at age ten. Today, I cannot make myself read or watch stories about the deliberate abuse of animals. And I am beginning to wonder what I can do for animals who have been so abused.

One of the things we learn at this stage of "Compassion" is that compassion for others is the best way to heal ourselves. When we let our soulful compassion guide us into action, we may find ourselves reaching out to others with a kind word, a note, or a helping hand. A friend, who has lost several cats in recent years and who is herself in poor health, is most grateful for the help of friends who have offered to dig the cats' graves. She, in turn, offered a burial place for a friend's kitty who had died. Compassion builds upon compassion, kindness upon kindness, and makes the world a better place.

One last thing about compassion. Compassion allows us to define who we are and what we expect from life. Once we have begun to experience compassion, we begin to realize that we do not want to live in a world that is devoid of it. That, in turn, gives us the opportunity to define ourselves as compassionate people and to commit ourselves to living compassionate lives, including compassion within the folds of our life purpose, whatever that may be. I once spoke with a woman from Long Island, New York, who spends her life as a physical therapist and caregiver for injured animals. Her mission is a difficult one, but she wouldn't trade her life for any other. So it is with a woman whose story I saw on television not long ago. She was a homeless person whose only real friend was her dog, and that experience inspired her to open and run an adoption shelter for dogs who, for whatever reason, were homeless. Her love and compassion have transformed her entire life.

When we reach the stage of compassion, the softening that takes place within our hearts paradoxically yields us the strength to define how we want life to be. We become more proactive. In the first two stages of our grief, we were feeling that life was dictated to us and that there was nothing we could do about our miserable fate. Now, we realize that we want the world to be a compassionate one (both for ourselves and for others), and we commit ourselves to making it so. Compassion has turned us around.

Stage Four: Tapestry

This is a story that I have told elsewhere, but it is worth repeating here. It's the story of a little boy whose mother was embroidering. Curious as to what she was doing, he came over to inspect her work. "That's ugly," he told her with great assurance.

The mother smiled. "You go off and play now," she said to him. "Come back later and see what I've done."

Later, the boy returned to his mother. To his surprise, she was holding a beautiful cloth embroidered with a lovely flower.

"Son," the mother said, "when you saw the cloth earlier, you saw it from underneath. All you could see was a jumble of threads of all different colors, and it looked ugly to you. From where you stood, you could not see that there was a pattern to all of that. That pattern produced this beautiful flower."

Until we learn to see with eyes of the soul, we see in ways similar to that of the little boy. We look and look, but what we see does not appear to be beautiful. We do not know that there is another side, and that on that side the very pattern we deemed too ugly appears very beautiful. That is what the soul longs to teach us. It is at the stage called "Tapestry" that we can begin to learn.

When we move into the stage of "Tapestry," we learn that the events in our lives are not the mere coincidences they seem to be. Like the little boy who at first saw only the ugly side, we gradually find ourselves looking again and seeing that there is another side to things. This can happen in any of several ways. Spend some time online putting keywords into Google, such as "animal loss," "animal grief," and "animal rescue," and you will find story after story of people whose experience of having lost an animal or having seen one abused has led them to dedicate their lives to helping fellow animal lovers and needy pets. These dedicated people discovered in a painful situation a whole new mission in life.

Discerning the tapestry in the loss of a pet may not take as dramatic a turn as that. One of the most healing things we can do in the aftermath of the loss of an animal friend is to write a poem or a story or paint a picture about him or her. You'd be amazed at how cathartic this can be. If you want to see some examples of how poignant this can be, there's a Web site at http://www.petloss.com/poems/poems.htm with numerous poems and stories written about the loss of a beloved pet. These poems and stories are written with the heart and the soul. They turn a heart-wrenching experience into meaning and beauty.

Writing stories or telling them or discovering a mission to help grieving humans and grieving and abused animals gives us a valuable piece of information about the heartbreaking experiences in our lives. They tell us that the moments of our lives, even the painful ones, can be teachers and guides for ourselves and for others. When we began our grieving in the stages of "Lost Soul" and "Falling Through the Cracks," we did not think that there was any meaning in our loss other than searing pain. In the stage called "Tapestry," we learn that telling our stories (honed but not yet expressed during the stage of "Compassion") can make things better for ourselves and for others. It reminds us to let our experiences guide and lead us and others to genuine wisdom.

There's something else about telling our stories that is really a fascinating tribute to the soul's magnetism. As we begin to tell our stories, we'll find ourselves drawing people into our lives who are kindred souls. If you looked at www.petloss.com, you have already drawn into your circle others who have had a similar experience to yours and a similar reaction to it. When I first started to let people know about the respective deaths of Lionel and Teddy, I was overwhelmed by the expressions of compassion I received. I think, too, we learn to put into a better perspective people who tell us to "snap out of it" because "it's only an animal." We tend to pay them less heed and, who knows, we may even find them passing out of our lives without our having to do anything.

Another fascinating aspect of "Tapestry" is that being at this stage creates in us a very different expectation about life than what we had before. Then, we were consumed by the belief that life was meaningless, a series of events to be described as "one darned thing after the other." Now, we find we are developing the expectation that life is meaningful even when painful; and we find ourselves more often looking for meaning in the events of our lives. This is truly a more inspired and inspiring way to live. Related to this, we begin to replace the idea that life is fickle with the idea that life is something that we can count on. Life can still be a struggle at times, but when we know the soul is always there for us, it makes a difference.

PRECIOUS DEAR AT HOME

Stage Five: Attic Wisdom

No, you don't have to learn Attic Greek to move into this section. This stage is not about an ancient language; it is about attics, the attic, perhaps, of your house. In *Stages of the Soul*, I called this stage "Attic Wisdom" because it is very much like the attic of a house, which is above the everyday living space in the home and contains discoverable treasures that are apart from the things used everyday. In our attics, we have old books and records we haven't read or heard in years. We have old photo albums reminding us of how grandmother and grandfather looked when they were married. We may find old toys, even clothes worn in days gone by, that bring back wonderful memories of our younger years. Attics are treasure houses.

In the stage of "Attic Wisdom," the soul moves beyond and through its heightened sense of compassion and moves to a higher level of reflection and insight. At this level, we are well beyond the imprisonments of grief and move instead to a place where we can sort through our memories and learn important things about life and about the place our animal companions have in it. In "Attic Wisdom," we take time to reflect, to discover the treasures that we may have buried and hidden away, and allow ourselves to be surprised, perhaps by what we learn.

Perhaps it's telling the stories of our animal companions that primes the pump that leads us toward "Attic Wisdom." Telling the stories of Peter and Bounce and Spike, for instance, unleashed a flood of memories about my childhood. Peter's story takes me back to the first apartment (a small three-room, third-floor place) in which my parents lived after they were married. Peter's song reminds me of my dad's old radio (not so old in those days), which I eventually had in my office years later when I was working in college administration. I think of my first books and listening to my mother as she taught me to read, and I remember her taking me for walks to see gardens and flowers. There were, of course, problems, as well, and there are those memories, too. But even there I find that there is an element of surprise in the discovery of those memories. I can learn from the painful ones and choose not to dwell excessively on them. I can treasure the happy memories and gladly realize that in my own case, I grew up in an atmosphere of love and safety that has been a touchstone of my life. Our animal friends and our memories of them open doors of remembrance that help us to get in touch with our deepest destiny. Our souls love to remember, and they love to learn and to teach through memory.

What is happening in this "Attic Wisdom" stage is that our soul is leading us and calling us beyond the everyday and inviting us to experience what is truly lasting. Wayne Dyer in his book *Inspiration* says that we are what we remember, and that these cherished memories help us to get a sense of our eternal purpose in unexpected and even delightful ways. When my friend Susan's cat, Kitty Taylor, was dying of cancer, I would go every night and cook her favorite meals (lamb and Mrs. Paul's breaded clam strips). Kitty Taylor and I were very close, and those meals (even though she often didn't eat them) seemed to bring her comfort and satisfaction. Remembering those moments, poignant though they were, reinforces for me the realization that part of my calling in life is to serve and love wonderful animal friends like Kitty Taylor.

That's part of the "Attic Wisdom," but there's more. The lesson here is not just about Kitty Taylor; it's also about love as an eternal value. It's about respect for animals and for the earth that we share. "Attic Wisdom" leads me beyond the realm of the particular, and, while including that, brings me up into the realm of the eternal.

"Attic Wisdom" also keeps us mindful that there are a whole host of ways in which to encounter the eternal. Not long ago, friends gave me the complete DVD set of James Herriot's wonderful *All Creatures Great and Small* as it was broadcast years ago on BBC. Though it is unlikely that I will ever be a country vet, watching this delightful series reminds me of why I love animals and gives me another avenue for keeping that love alive in my life. Often, people write to me to share their memories of their pets or to ask for advice about how to care for a needy animal. Those wonderful e-mails and letters also serve to keep me in touch with my love for animals and, through use, strengthen my ability to be of help to them. Recently, on the computer, I found a picture of an adorable yellow Lab puppy (with enormous jowls and paws), and I put him up as the wallpaper on my desktop. Though I can't have a dog right now, this delightful little fellow touches my heart and gives me joy.

"Attic Wisdom" can do something more for us, too. In the previous stage of the soul, we learned that there is a tapestry to our lives that might not always be apparent in our day-to-day living. In "Attic Wisdom," we get the opportunity to look beyond the tapestry to the One who is weaving it. I believe that our animal friends are gifts from God to us to keep us mindful of the beauty, the simplicity, and the love that is the essence of the divine and that is our birthright as creatures made in God's image and likeness. Experiencing them, remembering them, we remember God.

The idea of remembering God leads us to understand yet another dimension of our relationship with our soul. This realization is helped by the teachings of the Judeo-Christian scriptures, which tell us that our relationship with God is that of a covenant. A covenant is not a contractual agreement, nor is it a casual and spontaneous showing up from time to time in one another's lives. A covenant is a solemn mutual commitment of love between two or more people. Part of what is involved in that love is the promise that we who are entering into the covenant will always be there for one another. God promises to be there for us, and we promise to be there for God. In the stage of "Attic Wisdom," we learn that the soul is a place to which we can always come to embrace the presence of God. In difficult, painful, or confusing times, we can always return to the attic (metaphorically to the soul, to the presence of the divine) and find there safety and comfort, light and refreshment. We, in turn, promise to keep a place for God to dwell within us. This means taking deliberate conscious action to assure that the dynamics of inspiration will always be a part of our lives. It means taking time to meditate. It means taking time to be inspired by the beauty of nature (including the animals). It means looking for ways to share God's love with those in need (including the animals). In our houses, we can treat the attic as merely a storehouse of old items we no longer think about or want, or we can endow it with the magic of a storehouse of cherished memories. With our lives, we can treat our soul as something nice to think about once in awhile, when we're not thinking about the practical things we have to do. Or, we can cherish and nurture our soul, invite its wisdom, seek its guidance. The growth that we are describing here as we explore the dynamics of our grieving process suggests that the latter route is a better and more satisfying way to go. It's just deeper and more attuned to our true nature.

What it comes down to, I think, is making a habit of asking, "What do I really want in this particular situation in which I find myself?" We may initially think that what we want is a quick fix or a way to forget so that we can "bring closure" to our grief. Soulful living, however, suggests that what we *really* want is inner peace and light for ourselves and for others. The stage of "Attic Wisdom" helps us to find that.

KITTY TAYLOR, NY PENTHOUSE

Stage Six: Return

We have come far enough along in our journey through grief to come to the realization that the terribly devastating experience of losing a beloved animal need not lock us in to relentless pain and sorrow. A soulful approach to our bereavement allows us not to cut off the pain and suffering, but rather to experience it fully. At the same time, a soulful approach allows our sadness to teach us, to bring us to a higher level of inspired living, and in addition, shows us that the soul itself can be a valuable companion and guide. We do this by allowing the poetry and the mystery of the soul to draw poetry and mystery from the situation that once seemed so desperate and hopeless. We still miss our beloved pet. We still wish he or she were physically with us. But by allowing our experience to teach us, we come to a higher and deeper appreciation of ourselves, of our mission, and of life itself. This in no way diminishes the value of our relationship with our pet. Rather, it enhances a notion that has become very popular in animal-lover circles of late—the notion that our animals can be our teachers. Since Teddy was so very old, I knew for years that one day he was going to die. I am grateful that I anticipated that and made the most of every day and every moment we had together. When I woke up that April morning and found Teddy had gone, I was able to live without any regret of having left anything undone. Has Teddy's death taught me anything? Perhaps it's a little soon to say, but I think my greatest realization is how large the animal spirit can be. More than I realized, Teddy's spirit filled my home. Now that he is gone, there is a sizable gap in the spiritual timbre of the place. Yet I wonder, if his spirit were not somehow still present, would I feel the loss of him so much? Put differently, is it possible that the fact that I miss him, actually gives witness to the fact that he is somehow still present to me? I prefer not to engage right now in theological speculation about whether animals go to heaven. I suspect they do, but what if Teddy's heaven or your beloved pet's heaven were in my memory and in my heart? Wherever you or I go in the afterlife—hopefully to heaven—we will always take them there with us. In the spirit, they can never go away. The soulful memory will simply not allow it. Teddy, in his death, has taught me that.

Even in death, our animals are our teachers and our companions. There is something completely right about that.

I mentioned having no regrets with Teddy. That is not always the case when our animal friends die. Perhaps we feel we could have done more. Perhaps we wished we had been more observant. Perhaps we regret not being with them at the moment of their death. Perhaps we feel guilty about having had them euthanized. (This, by the way, is not "putting them to sleep." That expression soft-pedals what is a serious and portentous moment. We are helping a sick and dying animal transition from life to death. We should treat that moment for what it is and deal with it accordingly.) Perhaps we regret not having spent more time with them, or we regret a moment when we lost patience with them.

The best advice I have heard with regard to guilt in grief is to acknowledge our feelings of guilt and then let go of them. None of us is perfect. We all make mistakes. We all do things that later we regret. It makes no sense to clutter up the loving relationship we have had with our animals by giving in to relentless remorse. In life, they loved us unconditionally, and one of the things that animals as teachers can teach us is to love ourselves unconditionally as well. If, on reflection, we find we did make serious mistakes, then the trick is to learn not to make them in the future. That's the long and the short of it. Staying in guilt is pointless and, in fact, needless.

Having said all of that, there comes a moment when it is time to get on with life. This I call the stage of "Return." This, by the way, is not about bringing your loss to "closure." I have heard that expression so many times, and each time I find it to completely misrepresent the essence of the soulful grieving process. As we have been observing, the grieving process is not something that can be turned on and turned off like a water faucet. There is no "getting on with life" that does not include holding cherished memories of our faithful animal friends. There is and should be no closure to the relationship we have had with them.

It is much better, I think, to say that there comes a moment when the soul leads us out of the attic and back downstairs where life is being lived. We take with us the memories, the tender positive feelings, and the learnings from our time in the attic; but there comes a time when we need to get back to work. We may find that our work has changed. We may feel inclined to volunteer with animal welfare agencies or groups, or start one of our own. We may find ourselves wanting to get the training necessary to help others who are grieving the loss of a pet. We may find ourselves drawn to a new hobby or craft, such as telling animal stories or making jewelry with animal images. Or we may simply go back to our former life and decide that it is time to bring another animal friend home. Whatever our experience, we are changed. We know more about the relationships we have had with our animal friends. We know more about life and about ourselves. Once fraught with grief and despair, we now have hope in life. Our animals and our souls have teamed up to give us that. The really good news is, we always know where the attic is and are free to visit it whenever we wish. The soul's nudge to return to daily life is by no means an invitation never to go upstairs again. In fact, we need to go there on a frequent, if not daily, basis. Now we can do that and still live a full life here on earth. It's a very good deal.

Stage Seven: Re-Enchantment

I have long been a fan of the comic strip *Peanuts*. Some time ago, I discovered that I could get my favorite strip daily via e-mail. This morning, as I was sitting down to begin my day, there was today's *Peanuts* installment. It is spring, and baseball season is underway. The team—and most vociferously Lucy—is bemoaning the sad results of its most recent game. "Six hundred to nothing!" Lucy shouts at poor Charlie Brown. "It is your fault we lost. You're the manager! And when a team loses, it's the manager's fault! Six hundred to nothing! Good grief! Why didn't you use some *strategy?*" They walk away, leaving poor Charlie devastated.

Years ago, Robert L. Short came out with a book called *The Gospel According to Peanuts* (Bantam Books, 1964), the thesis of which is that themes from the four gospels could be found in the comics of Charles Schulz. If that's true, there's at least a life-lesson in this one. When things go wrong, we always blame the manager. Generally, we take that all the way up to God. The members of the team don't seem to consider the possibility that, despite the best intentions of the manager, they just didn't play well. Six hundred to nothing is a pretty bad performance. Maybe, just maybe, they had something to do with it. Or, maybe the other team was just a whole lot better. That's another possibility.

As we have gone through the various stages of the soul in our grief, we have probably found ourselves at some point or other blaming God for the loss of our pet. Somebody probably told you that your pet's death was "God's will" or that "God took him or her home," and you got mad. Mad at them, but also mad at God. As we have passed through the stages, we have looked honestly at the various possibilities. At times we've blamed ourselves, at times we've blamed fate or God, at times we have perhaps blamed the vet or someone else. We have learned how to soulfully handle each of those angers. We've learned not to let them get us into trouble, nor to just smile them away, but rather we allow them to teach us about life. Through the higher perspective of the soul, we have learned that we may not understand everything about why our pet died. We have learned, too, that we are not alone, that we probably did our best for our animal friend, and that if someone really was to blame, perhaps that can motivate us to be sure that animals (and our animals especially) get better care in the future. That might become our mission.

We've come a long way and have done a lot of learning, softening, and reflecting. We have even returned to the world, armed with our new perspective and our new knowledge. But it is not enough for us to simply return to the world. There is one stage left, and it is the most wonderful one of all. That is the stage where we fall in love with life again.

I called this stage "Re-Enchantment" for two reasons. One, I was taken with Thomas Moore's book *The Re-Enchantment of Everyday Life*

(HarperCollins, 1996), in which he so beautifully teaches us how to fall in love with life through noticing the everyday wonder in life. Two, the word "re-enchantment" comes from the French word *chanter*—to sing—and at this stage of the soul, we learn to sing again.

You see, it is one thing to return to life and quite another to be enchanted or re-enchanted with it. The two might indeed come simultaneously for us, but most of the time they don't. It is one thing to come back into life knowing more and having learned a lot. But it is not necessarily true that we come back to life singing. Can we make this happen?

I'm tempted to say the answer is "yes and no," but the truth is that the answer is really "yes and yes." Yes, the ability to return to life singing is a gift of which we must become the recipients, and yes, there are things we can to do open ourselves to receive that gift.

My belief and experience is that God wants to give us the gift of re-enchantment and that, indeed, he holds it out to us. There's another strain in *Peanuts* where Lucy holds the football for Charlie Brown to kick and then pulls it away when he goes to kick it, leaving Charlie in a heap on the ground. Some people get to thinking that that's how God or life acts toward them. I don't believe that for one minute. I see God holding out re-enchantment to us, and that he waits for us to accept it.

That's where the second "yes" comes in. We have to be ready for re-enchantment, ready and willing and able to accept it. We do that by making ourselves available for re-enchantment on a daily basis. In *Stages of the Soul*, I spoke of "stations of re-enchantment," places (literally and figuratively) where we can go to experience a deep sense of beauty and joy. It's important to note that we have to consciously go there—it's not enough for us to wait for them to come to us. These "stations" could be things like music or art or gardening or creating elegant meals or drawing or painting or fixing up the house, reading, knitting, helping at a soup kitchen, walking at the beach—whatever makes your heart fill up with joy. But the thing is, you have to do it—you have to create time and space in your calendar and make sure you go there. Becoming re-enchanted is a two-way street—God offers, but we must be open and we must create that openness on a daily basis.

I guess it's fair to say, too, that some stations of re-enchantment are not initially pleasant. I'm thinking of a friend who just e-mailed me saying that, at his doctor's insistence, he has taken up a regimen of daily exercise. Initially, this was not a pleasant thing for him; but he's staying with it and, as a result, he's feeling better. Nowadays, he doesn't jump for joy at the thought of exercising, although some day he might, who knows? Nonetheless, he's finding it an important dimension of his well-being. It counts as a station of re-enchantment, even though in and of itself, it's a difficult thing to do.

It's important to say one other thing about this stage of re-enchantment. It's essential to create both within and outside of yourself a sense of home. Like soul, home is a bit hard to define with any precision. Let me try it this way: home is where soul and earth meet. There, you are in touch with the best that your soul has to offer, and you arrange your life so that it reflects that soulful best. Another way to say it is: be guided from within and then have it the way you want it. There's an architect inside who will help you draw up the plans, and he also knows how to work those plans in your real life.

If that sounds impossible, all I can tell you is that it's not; people do it every day. Just don't get fooled into thinking that the best your soul has to offer is the best that the world tells you you must have. To put it in terms of animals, let me tell you a story about Lionel. When I was looking at Lionel at the Humane Society, he was an absolutely filthy dirty cat with a tattered ear. My friend who was with me kept trying to get Lionel to show himself off to me, but I was more interested in Suzie in the next cage, whose animal parent had died and who was deeply depressed. At that point, a mother and father and two huge teenage sons came in, searching for a cat to take home. Uh-oh, they were interested in Lionel. It looked like he was a goner. Just then, the mother pointed and in a horrified tone of voice said, "Oh, but look at his ear!" and walked out, husband and sons in tow. That cinched it. Lionel came home with me.

Now here's the point. That family was obviously conditioned (probably by a whole host of influences) to believe that beauty and acceptability (at least in pets) amounted to being physically perfect. Lionel wasn't perfect, and so out they went. Here's the other point. If I had missed Lionel, I would have missed the world. I got him home, started working on the ear with prayer and healing energy and, yes, it straightened up a great deal. He was filthy in the shelter; at home, he cleaned himself up (he did it all by himself) until he was the cleanest kitty I ever saw. My year and a half with him before he died (he was a very old boy) was the best time ever. I thank God that somehow he had instilled in me the realization that beauty and physical perfection did not necessarily go hand in hand.

So when you're getting re-enchanted, when you're working with your inner architect to plan your outer world, remember—the world doesn't always know what's really the best. Really be guided from within. Be discerning and don't necessarily be taken in by what "everybody" says. Ask those wonderful people who look after sick dolphins or who care for elderly and abandoned zoo elephants whether they would trade their lives for all the tea in China. Their answer will be a resounding no. Build your world the way you want it, but remember—having things without love and service will not lead to re-enchantment.

Speaking of Lionel, let me mention that one of the important stations of re-enchantment in my life is the place on my bookshelf where I have photos of the cats who have come and gone from my life. Having those pictures to look at fills my soul with gratitude and reconnects me with the love each of those animals and I shared. I smile when I see those pictures. There is Flicka as a kitten, before I knew her. You could have predicted that she would grow into those enormous paws. There is Lionel, looking proud as a little lion. Soon Teddy will join them in the hall of fame. For now, I have left Teddy's blankets and the futon and the doggy-steps I bought him, left them where they were when he used them. For now, they are my stations of re-enchantment that keep me connected to Teddy's indomitable spirit.

I must say, Dear is a station of re-enchantment for me. She is still very sad over Teddy's death, but when she comes up to me and rubs my legs or hops up into my lap, she and I comfort each other. I've noticed that she is starting to imitate things Teddy did; I guess she's trying her best to keep him alive in her heart. Yesterday, she climbed up on Teddy's blanket (where he slept just before he died), snuggled into it, and tucked her head under her paws the way Teddy did. She amazes me.

Be free and creative about your stations of re-enchantment. The good news is that, contrary to what you thought when you were a lost soul and falling through the cracks, you can enjoy life again.

LIONEL FRANKLIN

Part Two:
Soulful Musings

Introduction

Years ago, when I was hosting a weekly radio program called *As You Think*, I interviewed a woman by the name of Stephanie Ericsson, a young widow, who had written an excellent book on grief called *Companion Through the Darkness* (HarperCollins, 1993). Talking to Stephanie, I remarked on the brevity of each of the chapters in her book. "When people are grieving," she told me, "they don't have the energy to read huge volumes of material. They need short pieces they can read easily and without a great deal of effort."

I think the same can be said for those of us who are grieving the loss of our pets. We need to understand the stages of grief we are going through to gauge where we are and to see that something else lies ahead. At the same time, we need chapters that are short, simple, and practical. We need some of those "stations of re-enchantment" that I mentioned earlier. For while we're grappling with the reality of death and trying to stay in touch with our soul, very practical matters and considerations come up. These are the very things that may nag at us, distract us, and keep us distraught.

In the following chapters, I want to touch very simply and very briefly on a few of the considerations that inevitably come up when a beloved animal dies. They are intended as suggested ways of thinking about these things. They are not to be taken as a final answer to a problem. Each of us finds his or her own ways of dealing with the issues that come up when an animal dies, but having someone else touch on them can prime the pump, so to speak, that will get the consciousness flowing.

I begin with the story of Teddy, since his death occurred while I was writing this book. This is really Teddy's book in many ways, for by the time of his death, I had written a good deal of the book and had found myself stuck in it. Try as I might, the flow was just not there. When I found myself dealing with Teddy's death, everything opened up again, and I found myself inspired to write. So this is Teddy's book, and I begin this series of reflections with an essay on him. Perhaps you will be as touched by his soulfulness as I was during the twenty-five years of his life. I would be very happy if my reflections brought you to memories and reflections of your own, got your soul roiling with wonderful treasures of memory and feeling. Perhaps the best thing we can do for each other in a time of loss is to get each other to remember and to feel. If these thoughts do that for you, it would be my great pleasure.

Teddy's Legacy

I was in the process of writing this book when Teddy died. He passed away in his sleep in the middle of the night at the tender age of twenty-five, not a bad age for a cat, even a beloved one. Of course, I would have wished he could have stayed forever, but that was not to be. For eighteen years, Teddy had been my omnipresent companion, attaching himself to every aspect of my life—eating, working at my desk, sleeping, playing, and, yes, taking a bath. My baths were well supervised up to and including the last day of Teddy's life!

When I stop to think about it, it is a miracle that Teddy lived to be twenty-five. All his life, he was a sickly kitty. In one of my columns after Teddy's death, I reflected that one of the life lessons I have learned from being a cat-parent is that "there's no such thing as a free cat." Teddy came free, along with Flicka (his first "wife"), because some friends of a friend wanted to reduce their cat population from four to two. Why in the world they ever wanted to part with these two remarkable cats is still beyond me, and, as I have stayed in touch with one of their former owners over the years, I think he wonders, too. So it seemed like a good deal: I wanted a cat, I was getting two, and they were free. Little did I know that a month later, I would be rushing little Teddy to the animal hospital, where he had to have a portion of his large intestine surgically removed. The bill was staggering; so much for the "free cat." It was a close call, but Teddy recovered. Not long afterward, another vet diagnosed him with a feline form of chronic fatigue syndrome. Teddy had all the symptoms—he would be fine, then he would dehydrate, stop eating, and become nauseous and diarrheic. For a while, I would march him off to the animal hospital where they would monitor him, fill him with fluids, keep him for several days, and charge an arm and a leg. Eventually, I came to realize that I could just as easily care for Teddy myself, and for years and years nursed him through bouts of immune deficiency symptoms whenever they arose. In the last several years of his life, his health improved greatly, and in the last month or so his greatest problem was that he was having increasing difficulty using his legs to jump. He had been a magnificent jumper. For years, I could not shave in the morning without Teddy leaping into the sink to watch me—and also to nag for his food.

Teddy had the funniest little high-pitched naggy voice you ever heard in your life, and he knew how to use it when he was hungry. He would pace and whine and nag until you stopped what you were doing and fed him. Teddy had a remarkable capacity to monitor his nutrition. He would become visibly agitated if he saw that the supply of cat food cans in his drawer was running low. He insisted on variety, but his tastes in food changed without warning. When I came home from the store, he would know which bag contained his food, and he would supervise what I had bought.

Teddy was a talky cat, and I didn't know what I was unleashing on the universe when I encouraged him in this. It began when I started asking him, "Teddy, are you hungry?" and he would answer loud and clear. But only if he was actually hungry. If not, he wouldn't say a thing. I expanded his vocabulary by asking him when he was in my lap, "Are you all right?" and he would answer.

That's pretty much how it went until Flicka died. She died six years before Teddy, also at age twenty-five, and she and Teddy were together for over twenty years. She was a tough-looking and tough-talking Maine coon who ruled whatever roost she was in at the time. She and Teddy were like a couple. They fought together and played together, and at times even slept together. Teddy was a perpetual kid, and Flicka was his disciplinarian. Sometimes she would see Teddy's infractions, store them up on her internal scoreboard, and then one day smack him for no apparent reason!

When Flicka died, Teddy grieved. He watched from his window as I buried her, and over time began a daily morning ritual of sitting in the window where he could see her grave and cry loudly and audibly. This went on for the six years until Teddy died. It was a daily morning ritual. Dear, who came shortly after Flicka's death and did not know Flicka, eventually came to join him for this daily wail.

The morning ritual soon grew into an ongoing series of homilies or complaints (Lord knows what he was saying) that Teddy would deliver at the top of his voice, either from the open window where neighbors could hear him or from the sink in the bathroom. For all the world, they sounded like jeremiads. Over the years, Teddy found his voice. No offence to anyone, I hope, but I took to calling him Billy Graham. Teddy could have preached a revival. (Maybe it comes from being a preacher's kid.)

For all of his wonderful traits as a ball of universal love (I called him Teddy Bear because he looked like one), Teddy was a bit deficient when it came to brains. If you dropped food for him 180 degrees from where he was sitting, he simply couldn't find it. When Flicka was alive, I used to give them a treat called Pounce. Flicka adored it and would travel the world to get to it. Teddy thought it was supposed to walk to him. Yet somehow Teddy was smart enough not to know his name when he knew he was doing something he shouldn't. You could call him until you were hoarse and get absolutely no response. "Teddy" was temporarily not his name.

As I said, Teddy looked just like a Teddy Bear. He had a reddish-yellow coloring and a teddy bear's cute face. Until his later years, when caring for himself became too much of a chore, he was terribly vain about his appearance. This was especially true of his tail, which was huge and feathery, blond and white-tipped, gorgeous. Teddy loved his tail. If a friend came to visit, I would say to him, "Teddy, show Irene your pretty tail." Up would come the tail, ready for admiring and adulation.

One other point about Teddy's coloring—this you're not going to believe, but it's absolutely true. All his life, Teddy was the blond color that I mentioned—until Lionel came. Lionel was a very old cat—the Humane Society tried to tell me he was nine. I say triple that. Lionel was Methuselah-old, had escaped somehow from his home, and was found between New York City and Connecticut. I was a bit worried bringing him home because he had Teddy's coloring, and I wondered what this might trigger. Little did I imagine. A couple of days after Lionel arrived, I looked at Teddy, only to discover that—what to my wondering eyes—Teddy's coloring was now reddish. I have never heard of anything like this happening, and if I hadn't seen it with my own eyes, I would swear I had gone crazy. Somehow, he had developed a shade of red in his fur so that no one would confuse him with Lionel! Wonders never cease.

It's very lonely these days without Teddy. Dear is grieving terribly, but coming along each day. Life definitely feels quieter and indeed off-balance without the little bear. I must say, though it was very difficult to watch him failing in the final couple of months, I truly treasured the experience of taking care of him and making his life as comfortable as possible during his final days. When it was looking like he wouldn't be able to jump up to his favorite spot on the sofa, I bought him some puppy steps, which he greeted at first with total disdain and then relented and used happily. Toward the day—which thankfully never came—when he wouldn't be able to climb at all, I bought him a little pet futon so that he would have a comfortable place to lie on the floor. Again, initial disdain was followed by delighted acceptance. To his dying day, he was never unable to demand his food. When he had trouble maneuvering the footstool to get up into my lap, I would pick him up, kiss his little head, and yell "Peter Pan" and "fly" him up to my lap. It was a wonderful time of making this beloved little fellow happy as he aged. I will treasure it always.

As his last Monday went on, Teddy failed visibly throughout the day. He made it up onto the couch before I went to bed, and I sat and cuddled him before I went to sleep. I woke up at 2:30 AM and found him sleeping on his rugs next to the futon. When I woke up at 3:30 AM, I noticed he was in the exact same position as before. I checked, and, sure enough, my friend was gone.

I didn't know when I started writing this book that I would be one of its beneficiaries. I write it in memory of Teddy and in thanksgiving for the wonderful years we spent together. Our eighteen years of his twenty-five are moments I will always treasure.

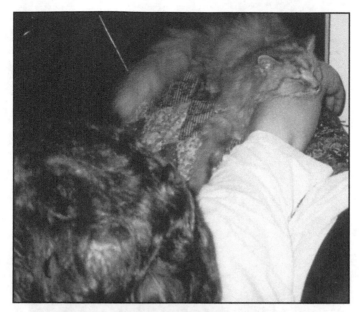

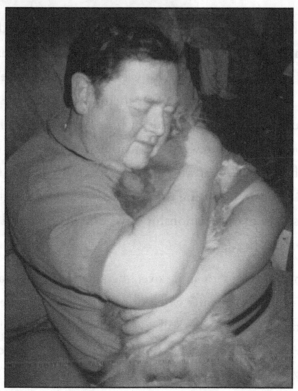

TEDDY BEAR & DADDY

Stories

When we are grieving the loss of a pet, we find ourselves telling stories about them. You'll find lots of stories in this book, because I firmly believe that telling stories is the best way both to honor their memory and to heal the pain that we feel over their loss. Telling the stories is a little like creating a scrapbook. Little by little, we paste the pictures into the scrapbook, and we preserve what otherwise might be lost. These stories are the treasures that we will take with us over a lifetime. Stories help us find a way to transcend the loss that we feel. Through them, we keep the best part of our relationship alive, and in a very real sense keep them alive in our hearts.

Our stories help us to smile over the smallest things, and indeed they give us reasons to smile when our hearts want to cry. I'll always remember our Boston terrier Spike waiting for me at the living room window every day before I came home from school. I remember how he would wag his little screw-tail because he was so happy to see me. I remember how my then-twenty-five-year-old Flicka, two days before she died, got up on my lap and stole an entire steak off of my plate—something she had never done before in her life. I remember how Kitty Taylor loved breaded clams—if the breading was removed from them *and only if* they were Mrs. Paul's. No other brand would do.

Though I find that my feelings over their loss never go away, the stories keep them living in my heart. These furry friends from my past continue to make a contribution to my life, even though they have been gone many years.

Treasure the stories. Tell them. Write them down, paint them, or turn them into music. Their stories make our friends eternal.

Pets in Heaven?

"Will I see my dog or my kitty in heaven?" This is probably the question I am asked most frequently by people whose pets have died. They have loved their pets through life and death, and they wonder whether they will ever see them again.

My answer is always, "Yes." I have had so much experience of the timelessness of the bond between humans and animals that I believe that I will see my animal friends again, and that you will, too. I think of Pope John Paul II's statement that heaven is a spiritual, rather than a physical, place, and I recall that the love between us and our pets remains in our hearts where it can never be destroyed.

I realize that I am saying this through the eyes of faith, and that I cannot prove that this is true. Yet it is what I believe. I remember holding my ancient kitty, Lionel, for three hours while he ended his battle with cancer, diabetes, and Cushing's syndrome. All the while, I talked to him, prayed aloud, and read Scripture passages to ease his final journey. I finally told him that I wanted him to stay, but if he needed to go, it was okay. With that, he sighed and passed away. At that very moment, the wind began to blow in the trees. I cannot prove to you that his was a spiritual journey, but my faith tells me that this is so.

If we can keep the love between our pets and ourselves alive in our hearts through memories and stories, it makes sense to me that their essence will be alive in our souls when we pass away. Children especially need to know about that love. The loss of a pet is for them a frightening thing unless we guide them. They need to know that they can always love their departed pets and that this love need never pass away.

Should I Get Another Pet?

"No more pets! I'm never getting another pet. It's just too hard to lose them." A woman sobbed those words to me a few years back on a radio talk show I was hosting. Having loved and lost several animal friends myself, I knew what she meant. I also knew that she wasn't expressing a commitment right then and there, she was really expressing her deep grief. When she had calmed down a little, I decided I would try to plant the seed of a new thought.

"If you think about your cat," I suggested, "do you really want her legacy to be that you would never get another one? Wouldn't a better legacy be that she opened your heart to want to provide a home for animals as long as you can?" It was a different idea, and I just planted it and let it lie. I knew it was probably too soon for her to get another one, but I wanted her to realize that down the road, she still might.

When to get a pet after losing one is a very personal decision. Many times people need to wait and give themselves a chance to heal. A rebound kitty might work about as badly as most rebound marriages. It can end up being a huge mistake.

After Flicka died (at age twenty-five), I did get another cat right away; and it was the best thing I ever did. The circumstances were unusual, though. Flicka died suddenly, and though I was aware of her advanced age, her death was shocking. The day after her death, one of my very closest friends also died, totally unexpectedly, of a heart attack. It was one sudden death on top of the other. I was in shock at how my world could change so rapidly in so short a time. I was also concerned about Teddy, Flicka's long-time companion. She and Teddy were like a couple, and I was concerned about his being alone. I decided, more or less on instinct, that, after all that death, I had better get some life into the situation. On the spur of the moment, I went to the Humane Society and in thirty seconds bonded with the most beautiful jet-black, green-eyed kitty I had ever seen. I took her out of her cage and held her in my arms and, as she snuggled into me, she began playfully exploring, with her keen eyes, the neon lights above her. I knew she was saying, "I want you to know I'm cute and cuddly, but I'm also going to be a handful." I brought her home, and she has been completely wonderful. She and Teddy became a couple, and she is largely responsible for keeping him young until his death at age twenty-five. Needless to say, Dear (she refuses to answer to Midnight) is the delight of my life.

It doesn't always work out that way, but it can. You have to just follow your instincts. If you're at all concerned that you might be moving too soon, I think it's best to wait. Your heart will tell you.

Speaking of Teddy, let me just say a word about other animals in the household. I knew Teddy pretty well, and he was fine with the new kitty. When deciding about the timing of adopting a new animal, it's good to take the personalities of your other pets into account. If they are pretty unsettled and disrupted after the death of a pet, it might be best to wait. Animals, too, need time and space to grieve. One of the reasons I like adopting from shelters rather than going to pet stores is that you can find out a bit of the history of the pet. One key factor is, do they get along with other animals? If they don't, and you have other pets, beware. Often it's good to know a little something about the breed. Do they tend to be edgy or nervous? Do they do well with children? Will they have too much energy for an older person to manage? These sorts of questions are important to answer when considering a new pet, and especially after one has just died.

DEAR

Helping Animals Grieve

The process of grieving the loss of your pet is not restricted to you alone. It may come as a surprise that your other pets may also be in mourning over the loss of their companion. Indeed, the extent of their grief can sometimes be amazing. When Flicka died, Teddy clearly grieved, but he was helped greatly by the arrival of little Dear. As the weeks went by, I began to think that things were back to normal. But on Thanksgiving Day, I noticed that Teddy seemed sad and listless, I would even say mildly depressed. It occurred to me that this was the first major holiday that he was without her. How he knew the day and why it seemed so different to him were beyond me. The same thing happened again at Christmas. It was a great lesson for me in the subtleties of animal grief. I mentioned earlier Teddy's morning ritual of going to the window by where Flicka was buried and spending some time there, sometimes crying. Especially, I noticed when the weather was bad, he would stand and watch over her gravesite as though he was worried about her. I learned to just let him be and occasionally try to reassure him. I know he missed her, and I think he understood that someday he would be with her again.

As I am writing this, my friend Susan's fifteen-year-old Tabby has just died due to complications from a tumor. Angel, Susan's remaining cat, who was not that well disposed to Tabby for most of her life, is very needy now of attention and affection and sometimes seems very sad. Susan is very wisely spending more time with Angel, comforting her, hugging her. That's the way to do it. It's important to pay attention to the remaining pets, to allow them to grieve, to notice their grieving, and to comfort them. Their grief is every bit as real as ours, and when we comfort them, we find ourselves being comforted as well.

Telling Children

I was three years old when one morning I went to the cage and found our beloved canary, Peter, lying flat on his back, feet up, dead. Needless to say, it was a shocking experience, and in some ways I didn't know what to make of it. I hadn't expected it—he had been fine the previous day. I was greatly helped by the fact that my parents dealt with me very straightforwardly about Peter's death and gave me a sense of peacefulness and reassurance around it. I had already experienced the deaths of my Grandmother Keenan (whom I did not remember) and Grandpa Cox (whose death and dying I was present for), so I was not completely unfamiliar with death. My parents had been very careful to reassure me about them, to keep their memory active, and to let me know that they were well in heaven. For that reason, they were able to deal honestly with me about Peter's death, to help me see that, though sudden, it was a natural part of life, and that I was not to be afraid. That calm reassurance has helped me to deal with so many deaths I have experienced since.

At the loss of a pet, each child will grieve differently. Some will be quiet. Some will cry. Some will be angry. However they express their grief, it is very important to reassure them, to be honest with them, and to help them to understand that death is part of life. They need to know that they can keep the memory of their pet alive, and keep their love for him or her alive in their hearts as a permanent treasure. It may be helpful to allow them to take part in a burial for the pet, or at least to memorialize him or her in some way. It's important to know that children will take their cues from the way they see us reacting. I was so greatly helped by my parents' way of handling Peter's death. I'm sure they had their own time for grief, but with me they handled it in such a realistic, comforting, and reassuring way. For that I will always be grateful.

Preparing for Death

Sometimes death comes very suddenly. I have been in the waiting room at the animal hospital when a family has come rushing in with their dog or cat wrapped in a blanket, hoping against hope that the accident will not prove to be fatal. It breaks my heart every time I see it. Yet there are many deaths that we can prepare for. Having had two cats live to twenty-five, I have learned to treasure every moment of their lives while at the same time staying aware that each day could be the last. In a way, it doesn't make it easier, and yet in another way it does.

What I am about to tell you is the most unusual thing I have ever experienced along these lines, but it's true. Flicka, my twenty-five-year-old Maine coon, died peacefully, suddenly, and, I am convinced, with full awareness of what she was doing. Six months before her death, Flicka began to prepare us for her dying. Little by little, she began to separate herself from Teddy. All his life, Flicka had been his friend, his mate, his disciplinarian. Yet over the last six months of her life, Flicka spent more time alone, and when Teddy approached her, she would hiss at him and shoo him away. Poor Teddy would look so brokenhearted and forlorn. I was bewildered. Yet looking back, I believe that Flicka was trying to prepare him (and perhaps herself) for the time when she would no longer be there. She did the same with me toward the end. All her life, Flicka hated to have her paws touched. Sometimes, playfully, I would touch her paw lightly with my finger and say, "What's this?" Flicka had a temper, and whenever I played "What's this?" I could be sure to get a good wallop from her enormous paws. A couple of days before she died, to my amazement, she came up and put her paw on top of mine, as if to beg me to play the game. The import of that didn't dawn on me until later. It was as if she knew she was going to go, and wanted one last game. At about the same time, she did something that she had never done before in all of her long life. Two nights before her death, I cooked a steak and sat down in my chair to eat it. For some reason, I looked away, and when I did, Flicka hopped up and stole the steak right off of my plate! It was so unlike her to do that, I just shook my head in amazement. Two days later, on that Wednesday night, she ate her dinner normally, went off by herself, and died. Flicka loved to eat, and it was fitting that she finished her dinner before she went. Looking back at everything, I began to see that she had been preparing herself and us for her inevitable passing. That may sound foolish, but I know my cat, and Flicka was definitely smart enough, self-determined enough, and wise enough to do it. She lived on her own terms and died on her own terms. It was her way.

I'm far from suggesting here that we should allow ourselves morbidly to dwell on death. But I am suggesting that we should always be aware of it, and even be open to the possibility that our pets may be trying to teach us about their death. It's a part of the beautiful bond we have with them. For me, at least, it enables me to treasure every precious moment with them and to enjoy the wonderful gifts their lives can bring.

Burying Your Pet

Burying Flicka, when she died, was one of the most difficult things I have ever had to do. It was a real moment of saying good-bye. It did not make it easier that Teddy watched from the window while I wrapped her in a blue towel, put her in a box, and lowered her into the ground. For me, burying and remembering my deceased animals has been an important ritual. It's not something that you can impose on anyone, however. We always have to remember that people grieve in different ways and need different rituals to comfort them. I'm convinced that we all need something, however. Our losses beg to be ritualized.

The rituals vary. Some bury their deceased animals on the grounds of their home. Others prefer to take a plot in an animal cemetery. Still others have them cremated, and either scatter their ashes or keep them in a safe place. Whatever custom you find comforting, it is really helpful to create some sort of ritual. It is a very important part of saying good-bye. Just as with our beloved family members, there is a kind of closure that comes with burial. When it doesn't happen, something is missing. We feel incomplete. Even if you decide to leave the body of your deceased pet at the vet's or at the animal hospital, it is really a good idea to create some sort of memorial. Our animal companions are precious, and we need to honor the contribution they made to our lives. The memorial can be a simple stone slab or something more like a tombstone, depending on your tastes. I keep pictures of my animals around my living space. Flicka's first "father" recently sent me pictures of her as a tiny kitten, with those huge paws just waiting to be grown into. I had it framed, and it sits in a gallery along with Lionel as a happy reminder of the girl I called "my Bunny Rabbit." Old snapshots of our Boston terrier, Spike, help me to enjoy his wonderful personality all over again. They gave us so much. It's important to remember them.

BABY FLICKA

Dealing with People

Whether the loved one is a human or an animal, one of the most difficult aspects of grieving is dealing with the well-meant but sometimes really annoying comments people make. It seems that in this regard there are two kinds of people: those who stay away because they don't know how to handle death, and those who don't know what to say but insist on trying. Actually, there is a third kind—those who know how to be present and what to say. They are precious.

Under no circumstances listen to people who tell you to get over it, that "it's only a cat/dog/horse after all," and that there are lots of people who are worse off than you are. For the most part, these things are not said out of malice but because people often don't know what to say in the face of loss. Remarks like that can raise your dander, and rightly so. There's nothing wrong with a strong reaction, but be really sure you want to harm your relationship. There's nothing wrong with saying, "Well, to me, Sammy was not just a dog; he was a friend and family member. While I know other people have worse losses, this one is pretty bad, and I'm feeling it." That honors your feelings without being insulting, and I often think that's the best way.

To the extent you can, try to surround yourself primarily with people who are understanding of your feelings. Feel free to limit, at least temporarily, your contact with people who do not. This is a time to be good to yourself, to give yourself the things you need, the time you need, the people you need. Take care of you. It might be a good time to talk to other genuine animal lovers who have been through this and who understand. It's certainly not out of line to seek out bereavement counseling if you feel that is appropriate. Many vets and most animal hospitals can give you referrals to counselors who specialize in grieving the loss of a pet.

Vacation Losses

When we speak about losing a beloved animal friend, we are usually talking about loss through death. But there are other ways of losing a pet. One of these is when we go on vacation and find that we cannot, for whatever reason, take our beloved friend with us, and we have to make arrangements for them.

Leaving an animal behind, though it is a temporary loss, is still a loss, and it may be extremely sad and even traumatic. My memories of this center around Spike, the Boston terrier we had when I was a kid. My parents often took long driving trips at vacation time, and it was necessary to board Spike in a kennel. We would be away for two weeks at a time, and, though nobody knew it, I was absolutely beside myself with grief over being separated from him. I was probably twelve at the time, and I can remember lying in my bed at night in the hotel room crying and talking to Spike, assuring him that I loved him and that we'd be together soon. I was a kid, and I think this is really a caveat for parents who board their pets while traveling. Parents need to be aware of the fact that leaving a pet behind can cause considerable sadness to a child. Especially when the child has nothing to do with the decision to be away and about boarding the pet, the situation might feel like nothing but loss and abandonment. Parents need to be sure that the child understands that the pet is safe and will be okay. And above all, parents ought to be aware of the feelings of their children about leaving the pet. If their feelings are anything like mine, is there a way to let them know that their feelings are appropriate, that you understand them, and that you will do everything in your power to make sure the pet is safe and happy? If it seems like the experience is going to be too traumatic for the child, consider doing something else for vacation, or finding an animal-friendly hotel or motel to stay in. What I am saying, really, is plan the experience beforehand, don't wait until the last moment to decide to involve the child in the process. I can tell you first-hand that doing it that way does absolutely no good at all.

Friends of mine who have two beautiful dogs and travel a great deal to various parts of the world engage the services of a dog-sitter. It's always a little risky, but they check the person out very carefully beforehand. They get references. They tend to choose someone who is nearby. They have an interview to see how the person interacts with the dogs and vice versa. They make sure the person knows what the preferred course of action would be in case of an emergency. My friends had one serious problem on one occasion with leaving the dog in the hands of someone they thought was capable (and whose services they had used before), but by and large it has been a good way to go. The dogs have the advantage of being in their own home and of receiving personalized care. My friends go away with the feeling that the animals are safe.

In this, as in so many things, be sure to listen to your heart. Even if you are an adult, you may have great anxiety leaving your dear animal friend behind. Honor your feelings. Think of the possible options, including taking your pet or pets with you. Be sure to check out thoroughly any kennel or boarding facility where you may consider leaving your animal. Visit it, meet the caregivers, check references. Leaving beloved animals behind can be traumatic, but there are ways of reducing the stress and grief.

Groups to Help and Support You

By now, I hope it is clear to you that grieving the loss of a pet is a normal thing, not a "crazy" thing or a foolish thing. Everyone grieves in his or her own way. Some people prefer to be alone and to take comfort in quiet reading, praying, and reflecting to heal their sense of loss. Others are more extroverted and prefer to be in a group. It is essential that during this time you get what you need.

If a group is what you need, there are many options available. Almost everywhere these days, there are bereavement counselors who assist people with all kinds of grief. With the Internet so prevalently helpful these days, it is not difficult to find a bereavement counselor in your area. Many houses of worship these days offer bereavement counseling, and bereavement groups meet in many churches and synagogues to help people who are experiencing loss. One of the great blessings of living in these times is that bereavement is taken much more seriously than in the past. We now have trained counselors and groups to facilitate the process of healing.

Beyond that, there are counselors and groups who are specifically trained in helping people who have lost pets. I think this has arisen because people grieving animals have felt uncomfortable being in groups where the majority of people are grieving spouses, children, and friends. They worry that those who have lost human loved ones will perceive their loss as trivial. The best way to find a counselor or a group who can help you with the loss of a pet is to call a veterinarian, a local animal medical center, or a pet adoption agency. Animal lovers love to network, and these centers of professional care for animals are often excellent sources of information. Some vets and many animal hospitals have either a referral or someone on staff who does bereavement counseling for pet losses. Usually, it's just a question of picking up a phone to ask.

Restoring a Sense of Wonder

One of the debilitating effects of grief is that it makes the whole world seem gray or dark. When we're mired in sadness, life loses its luster and sparkle, and we lose our sense of curiosity. We need to wonder. Without wonder, life is bleak, and we begin to wallow in the sense that there is nothing left in life for us. We begin to feel badly about ourselves, and we lose all sense of any joy or purpose in life other than to get through the day.

Even when we're in the early stages of grief, where we are caught up in the darkness of our situation, we can find ways of restoring wonder. One of the best ways is to begin to wonder at the process that we are going through. I am writing this in the midst of the loss of Teddy, and I often find myself fascinated about the grieving process and how I am going through it. One of the good things about determining to go through our mourning in a soulful way is that we develop the sense that we are being guided through a process rather than just randomly passing from stage to stage and reaction to reaction. Another thing is that we can step back and observe the process, for the soul both allows and invites us to do that.

Hindus have known this for years. They speak of the Observer, which lets us step back from our experiences and watch them as they unfold. Stepping back, I can see my wonderful memories of Teddy, and alongside them the daily reminders of how much I miss him. Sometimes it's very hard to talk about his death; at other times I can do it quite easily. I often feel that I am standing on a riverbank, watching the current take its various twists and turns, alternately going deep and shallow and sometimes swirling with rapids. Because I can sit back and watch, I know what is happening, and I can wonder at its twists and turns. I am often astonished at the various colors of the grieving process.

I also find myself in wonder over the way Dear is grieving. Some days she just cries and clings to me. Other days she plays hockey with her little plastic balls. Sometimes she just curls up in Teddy's old blanket and goes to sleep there. At other times, she goes to the window and, crying, holds vigil for Teddy as she observes where he is buried. I don't believe she can observe the ebbs and flows of her grief, but I can, and they are fascinating.

Wonder can be fueled by a myriad of things. While grieving, don't hesitate to put yourself into nature to experience its beauty. Look for sunrises and sunsets. If you can, find someplace where you can watch rabbits and squirrels play. Let your soul be caught up in the beauty of a cloud, a tree, or the flight of a bird. Make your way to a tall mountain, a desert, a beach, a lake, or an ocean. Go back and read a favorite story, book, or poem. These intimations of beauty allow you to acknowledge that you live in a wider reality than the confines of your grief. That doesn't mean denying your grief. It means living it with a sense of its place in the larger scheme of things.

To do this is to allow ourselves to wonder. Another name for wonder is "astonishment." When we can allow ourselves room for astonishment, we are more readily able to deal with the darker side of mystery as well.

TEDDY & DADDY, 1999

Euthanasia

This is one of the most difficult parts of animal parenting to talk about and, of course, to do. Nonetheless, it is an important aspect of loving our animals, and all I can do is address it, unhappily or not.

Let me say at the outset that while, under certain circumstances, I condone euthanasia for animals, I do not condone it for humans. That doesn't mean that I believe that every possible extraordinary means of keeping a human being alive should be tried. My norm is that they should be given food and water, as a minimum, and other forms of treatment are optional. Food and water allow the body to live naturally until it is ready to die naturally. But why is euthanasia permissible for animals and not human beings? My personal answer comes from my Christianity. I do believe that, thanks to the suffering, death, and resurrection of Jesus Christ, human suffering can be redemptive; that is, it can bring good to the soul and to the world. I do not believe, however, that the suffering of animals can be redemptive in the same way. Their soulfulness is of a different order than ours, and I do not think their suffering can bring goodness to them or to the world. Therefore, under certain circumstances, I believe it is permissible to perform euthanasia on animals but never on humans. Depending on your beliefs, you may have a different point of view, but this is mine.

When I say "under certain circumstances," I mean that the suffering of the animal must be apparently irreversible; that is to say, there is no reasonable hope of the animal's recovering. (Note that I say, the *suffering*, not necessarily the illness, must be irreversible. Many animals live with illnesses, just as we do, but their treatment is such that the illness does not produce great suffering.) To be more specific, I do not condone euthanasia merely because the animal is old (I have had four wonderful older cats whose lives I treasure) or merely because the treatment is inconvenient or costly (there are always second opinions and options for treatment). I most certainly do not condone euthanasia when it is "inconvenient" to keep the animal. There are plenty of animal shelters and clinics available to care for sick, injured, and unwanted animals. Euthanasia merely for the sake of convenience is utter disrespect for animal life.

When the suffering is irreversible, and the quality of life is seriously impaired, then euthanasia can be an option. It is probably one of the most painful things we ever have to do as animal parents. As of now, I have not had to do it myself, although animals have died naturally in my arms. If you find yourself in this situation, try to be present for the animal if you can, hold him or her if you can, thank them for their life with you, bless them, and let them go. Your heart will surely break, but realize that you are doing this for the animal's best interest, as part of your loving care for them.

If, reading this, you remember having had an animal euthanized and are wondering if you did the right thing, the best thing to do is to learn from any mistake you might have made, but don't spend a great deal of time loading yourself up with guilt. You likely did the best you knew how to do at the time, and if you find that you would do it differently today, then you have learned something. You still are a good, responsible animal parent. Just do better the next time.

Opening Up

A time of grieving often feels like a time of shutting down. There's a part of you that just feels like it has closed off to life. Often, people feel heavy, alienated from those around them and from the flow of life itself. Sometimes the flow of life seems slow and thick, like molasses.

While it's important to experience this feeling and not to cut it off, it's also important to take steps to ensure you don't simply succumb to the spiritual sluggishness. The secret to soulful grieving is to allow yourself to be in the moment just as you are, and at the same time to keep mindful that there is a larger reality that you can draw upon. In a very real sense, we are citizens of two worlds, and the only way to ensure that we do not get locked in to the more limited one is to keep ourselves exposed to the larger one. Jesus is reported to have said that you cannot serve two masters, and in this case it's really true. If we want to live fully, we have to do what we can to ensure that we are living in the realm of the soul and not being trapped in the limited perspective of ordinary thinking and experiencing.

When you're feeling trapped, one good thing to do is to breathe. I know, you're going to tell me that you never stopped breathing, but that's not what I mean. I'm talking here about the breathing that opens up the soul, takes us back to where we are our truest and best selves.

If you have meditated or heard anything about meditation, you know that, as esoteric as we often make meditating out to be, it often comes down to focusing our breathing. Many forms of meditation begin and end with inhaling deeply and exhaling deeply and getting the breathing into a slow rhythm. Some of the meditations say that by inhaling we are taking in new fresh air and by exhaling we are getting rid of all the negative stress and tension we have been holding inside us. Doing this for about five minutes can do wonders to put you in touch with your true self and learning to live from the soul rather than from the limitations of circumstances. Partly it's about "getting the cobwebs out," but that's really only half the story. The other half is that we open ourselves up to the soulful reality that is inside us, and from which we can learn to embrace new ideas, new possibilities, and, I am going to say as well, embrace God. For embracing God is really the point. As I said from the beginning, I am not looking for "perfect" ways to fix your grief. I am talking about letting your grief introduce you to a whole new way of thinking and being, a way that endows us with a depth and wisdom that perhaps we had no prior inkling of.

To do this, you do not need expensive equipment or a climb up the Himalayas. All you need to do is to get into a comfortable sitting or lying position, breathe in slowly and deeply, and breathe out. Do this for several minutes—your capacity to do this will increase as you become more used to it. In time, you'll become aware of a releasing of tension and a profound inner peace.

Some people catch on to this pretty quickly and do it fairly easily.

I find that for myself, I do better if I have a guided meditation tape of some sort. That just helps me to stay focused and not get distracted. The real "masters" of meditation go it alone. Oh well, I'll get there someday. There are plenty of good books and tapes out with guided meditations and lots on the Internet as well. You'll have no trouble finding something that is right for you.

You don't have to stay closed up forever. Meditative breathing opens up the closed doors and, as the old proverb goes, opens up new and better ones as well.

Use Your Grief as a Guide

On the particularly bad days when we are grieving, it's tempting to think that there is no way out of these miserable feelings and this miserable life. Perhaps we try this or that remedy, buy an assortment of things to take our mind off our troubles, or even just retreat into our slump. There's something else you can do, and it's so close to home that it may surprise you.

There's a man by the name of Joe Vitale who writes about marketing, often from a spiritual perspective. In his book *The Attractor Factor* (Wiley, 2005), Joe answers the age-old question, "How do I know what I want?" That's one of the most difficult questions for most of us, but especially, I think, when we're sad or grieving. It can be difficult to impossible for us to establish any kind of vision or plan for our lives. Joe's advice: start right where you are. You know what you don't want; now turn that around and change it into what you do want.

A lot of our ability to recover from loss has to do with vision. Is our vision limited by what we are currently experiencing, or can we see that there can be more to life for us? One way to get past the barrier of our sadness is to give our grieving its voice. Let my sadness tell me what I do not want in life. I don't want to be sad. I don't want to feel lost. I don't want to be without animals in my life, and so on. Write down in a list whatever your feelings are telling you. When you've finished, take your list and write the opposite of each item. That's what you do want. Just having that list can start you off in the right direction.

What's amazing about this is that it's so close to home. It's a good principle, in general, to start from where we are and to let our present situation guide us. I will say more about guidance soon, but for now, start with what you don't want, and let it take you to a vision of what you do.

Take It Easy

When we're grieving, whether for a human loved one or for an animal companion, we may find ourselves wanting to rush around trying to fix our feelings. Most of us are pretty good at trying to fix things. We have a deep abhorrence for things going wrong, and we like to put a great deal of effort into making things right.

There are a lot of reasons for this. We may feel guilty for what has gone wrong. In the case of the loss of a pet, we may feel we waited too long to prevent the death from occurring. If euthanasia was involved, we will almost inevitably feel guilty for having brought about the death of our pet, even though we know in our heads that there was nothing else to be done. Guilt is one of the most difficult emotions to put up with. As a result, we often try to eradicate, sometimes through food or alcohol or drugs, sometimes through intense bouts of activity.

Another reason we often feel badly about things going wrong is that at some level, it can make us feel that we are inadequate. We feel embarrassed and tell ourselves that if we were more competent people, this terrible thing wouldn't have happened. This is, of course, another aspect of guilt, and it, too, often results in our desperately wanting to hide our unconfident selves from others. Perhaps we become prickly or defensive, or, again, overactive.

The most important thing to do when these sorts of issues come up is to take it easy. Acknowledge what you are feeling, and release it. It's not doing you the least bit of good, and it is probably not telling you the truth about yourself. It's so important during the time of loss to be really gentle with yourself. If you discover that there are things you would do differently today, then you have learned something and that is a wonderful gift. Do whatever you need to do to protect yourself from feelings and people who would make you feel guilty or speak badly about you. You don't need to become defensive, but you also don't need to entertain them. In fact, here's a little secret that can help you a lot: once you are settled within yourself, those who would discourage or demean you will gradually disappear from your life, and more supportive thoughts and people will appear. You'll be amazed.

Why We Love Them So

I usually have a period of between two and three hours before going to work in the morning during which I think, meditate, read inspirational articles, and in general get ready for the day. One morning Sherman—at that time the newest feline member of my family—hopped up to the desk and sat down in front of me. I put his face in my right hand, and he proceeded to wrap his legs around my right arm while I was working. I actually had to control the mouse with my left (nondominant) hand. Come to think of it, I guess I had a cat in one hand and a mouse in the other!

This afternoon, I went to a nearby church to celebrate the noon Mass. Elio, the Italian handyman, was there. He's a favorite of mine, a gentle hardworking Italian immigrant who commands respect by his kindness. His English is heavily accented, and it's wonderful because he uses his hands to help his words along, and the whole effect is energetic. My friend Father Joe Baker, the parish priest there, mentioned my love of cats. Immediately, Elio's eyes lit up, and he launched into some wonderful stories about his cats, one of whom jumps up on his worktable every day to be brushed! The story I loved most of all was about the time Elio fell while doing a job and wrenched his back so that he was unable to walk. He went to the hospital, and they told him he was fine but just needed to rest in bed for a couple of days. From the time he got into the bed until the time he left it two days later, his little cat curled up on his legs and refused to move until Elio was well again.

Elio's story reminded me of Dear, who, whenever she senses that I am upset or not feeling well, is sure to come over and rub my legs or sit in my lap.

Then there was Rob Astorino's story. Rob is the program director at The Catholic Channel/Sirius 159 where I work. When Sherman was dying, Rob shared with me the story of Honey Bear, the dog who graced his family while Rob was growing up.

"We had a wonderful golden retriever named Honey Bear, who was just the sweetest dog. She was getting sick, and one day it became evident that she was laboring and time was running out. She went outside by herself for a while on a cold, snowy day (which she would always do because she was well trained) and stayed out for too long. We noticed she had collapsed in the snow and carried her back in. We put her on her favorite spot on the rug, and all of us just pet her and talked to her. She kept struggling to look up at us, and it was clear she was thanking us, and then she died with all of us around her. This was about fifteen years ago, and I still think of that moment and get teary."

Reading that story makes me teary, too.

Why do we love them so? Unless you already know, you don't know.

As my lawyer friend said on the train that night, "At what point did we cross the line into insanity?"

When I first had Teddy and Flicka, I hadn't been around cats much and found them fascinating. What amazed me was how readily they assumed a level of intimacy that most human beings would find unusual or even inappropriate. When I was still a kind of stranger to him, Teddy would hop up into my lap and snuggle there. No permissions, no hesitations, up he came and that was that. It was also amazing to me how readily they would allow me to be intimate with them. Due to an abusive situation in her previous home, Flicka trembled badly when I got her and even had trouble eating. She could be a force to be reckoned with, but she let me gently touch her and pray over her until at length the twitching stopped altogether. One morning she screamed when my foot hit the floor as I got out of bed. I picked her up and discovered a horrific anal infection. I rushed her to the hospital, and the doctor prescribed warm compresses three times a day for three weeks. I wasn't sure how Flicka would take to such treatment, but, no, she very gently sat and allowed me to administer her cure faithfully three times a day for three weeks. I was amazed.

SHERMIE on DADDY'S DESK

Why do we love them so? Because they touch our hearts so tenderly. On one level they are so helpless, so in need of us. On the other, they are so strong and independent and wise. They are images of ourselves, I think. They bring us out of ourselves and insist that we emotionally invest in them. It's the best investment you could ever make.

That's why when we lose them, we are so deeply saddened. How could we not be? A part of us has gone missing. It used to be there, we loved it, and now it is gone. Or so it seems.

I was speaking today with a woman who in the course of her lifetime has buried three adult children and a daughter-in-law. With deep emotion in her voice she said to me, "Of course, I haven't really lost them. They are always with me." I like to think that of my deceased animals as well. The pictures I have of them, the memories of their time with me, keep them alive in my heart. And that's a joyous thing, not a sad one. In my heart, they continue to enrich me, continue to fulfill their purpose for being in my life. Whether or not there is a heaven for them (and, as I said before, I think there is), there is certainly one for them in my heart. I never lose them. They are always with me.

Whatever stage of grieving might be yours right now, just know that there is a safe haven, a heaven, for your beloved pet in your heart. There they are always safe and happy, and you can visit them often and at any time. I pray that their passing may come to be a source of love and gratitude for you.

Epilogue:
From Shermie to Princess

I had no idea when I began to write this book that at the end I would be writing about saying good-bye to Shermie. My wonderful eighteen-year-old feline friend stopped eating just after Thanksgiving and within a week was dead from cancer. His death was fast, sudden, and unexpected. It was a heartbreaking loss. I thought losing Teddy was devastating. Shermie's passing was such a surprise and for me involved the loss of a great love.

I met Shermie on the Internet. Yes. He was on a Web site for an animal shelter, and he looked so forlorn in his little cage that my heart went out to him. I remember him sitting like a little ball of love on the floor of the house of his foster mother. When I saw Shermie for the first time, he weighed a mere four pounds. That was an improvement over the two pounds he weighed when he was rescued. It was impossible not to fall completely in love with him.

A friend actually adopted Shermie for herself, but as time went on, he stayed with me a few times, and we stole each other's hearts. So eventually, Shermie came to me and stayed with me.

Shermie loved two things: food and love. It soon became clear that Shermie was not the small kitty he appeared to be. Happily, he ate and ate and eventually made his way up to twelve pounds! He was the self-appointed monitor of any food that came into my place. He had a penetrating stare with which he would bore right through you until you gave him something to eat. There was no getting around that stare. Shermie made sure he had your full attention.

Love was his other passion. He loved to sit on my lap or on the top of my easy chair where I could rest my head against him. We would sit like that for hours on end. It's one of the things about Shermie that I miss.

As an old boy with a tough history, Shermie had multiple special needs. He had a hyperthyroid condition that required his taking a pill twice a day. Getting that pill into him was a daily battle royal until I learned from his foster mother that he loved baby food and would take his pill that way. That was fine, except for the fact that Shermie was very smart and learned how to enjoy the baby food while leaving the pill in his dish. In the end, I crushed the pill and fooled him into thinking he was just eating his Beech-Nut delight. It worked like a charm.

One of the things I remember most was our nighttime routine. I was working nights at The Catholic Channel, and when I came home, the first thing I did was to crush Shermie's pill and give him his baby food. Dear, of course, was jealous that he was getting something that she wasn't, so I would give her a bowl of milk. The routine was that Shermie would finish his baby food, lie down in front of Dear's milk bowl, and stare at her until she was finished—he wanted milk, too! Complicating this procedure was the fact that Dear, in an ornery moment, will sometimes choose the painfully slow method of drinking her milk drop by drop with her paw! So there would Shermie be, busting to get to the milk, while Dear took her own sweet time finishing.

The routine did not end there. Once he had had his milk, Shermie would hop up into my lap to be brushed. He had very dry skin and once had developed an itch reaction from the dryness. The vet suggested daily brushing, so after his milk, Shermie would hop up to be brushed, which he loved. I would tell him how handsome he was, and of course he would eat that right up! Once he was brushed, he stayed in my lap and went to sleep, as did I for the night.

Shermie's last days were heartbreaking, yet they were some of the finest days I had with him. A friend helped me care for him, which involved giving him intravenous fluids twice a day to keep him from dehydrating. He refused all food, and as the cancer in his belly grew, he wanted to be alone and to sleep. He distanced himself from me—I guess it was as hard for him to say good-bye as it was for me. As the vet said, there was nothing to do but keep him as comfortable as possible. So for a week, I was literally running a hospice. I have long said that I wanted to minister to and care for animals. In his own way, Shermie gave me a chance to prove that in his last days.

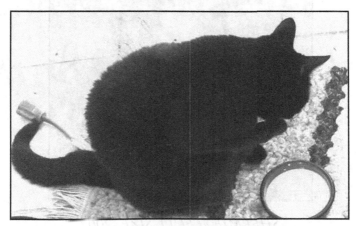

DEAR'S PAW METHOD

SHERMIE at FOUR POUNDS & DADDY, 2006

SHERMIE at FULL SIZE, 2007

During Shermie's last days, I had tremendous support from friends and colleagues, and when I was on the air, I was able to share with listeners what was happening with Shermie and received a tremendous outpouring of love and support from them. Shermie died while I was on the air, about a week after the onset of his illness. I think that's what he wanted; I sensed that he would go while I was out. My friend held him in his last moments, and he passed away.

As I said before, I had no idea when I started writing this book that at the end I would be discussing the loss of Shermie. I guess, in a way, the book was meant to help me as well as you. Like you, I find myself going through the stages and needing the stories in order to heal.

There was a dreadful emptiness when Shermie died, so dreadful that I wondered how one little cat could leave so large a hole. Not everyone would do what I did next, and each person has to decide for himself or herself when it is time to adopt another pet. Two days after Shermie died, I went to the Humane Society and adopted Princess, a beautiful three-year-old white and black kitty who brings so much joy to my life and makes me laugh every day. She and Dear are play pals, and every night when I come home from work, my two girls are there waiting for me with a wonderful greeting.

I miss Shermie terribly, but I am healing, and life is going on. It will for you as well, I promise. I hope this book will help you, as it is helping me, to deal with the loss of your beloved pet and to know that their real legacy to us is the love that even death cannot take away.

PRINCESS "HONEY," 2009

A Final Note

The loss of an animal friend is, in some ways, a never-ending story. As I said before, I do not like the idea of bringing any grieving to closure, for our loved ones always live on in our hearts. It is my sincere hope that the essays in this book have made your grieving process a bit less lonely and more soulful. If so, that makes me very happy.

I hope, too, that this book has helped you to treasure your own stories of your animal friend or friends. If you would like to share them, you can write a tribute at http://www.fatherpaul.com.

I wish you all the best as you go through this experience of loss. I hope and pray that it may expand your heart and soul into a deeper experience of soulful living.

Blessing of the Animals

During the Feast Day of St. Francis of Assisi on October 4 every year, churches around the world participate in the blessing of the animals.

This original blessing prayer by Father Paul Keenan appeared in *Pet Prayers & Blessings: Ceremonies & Celebrations to Share With the Animals You Love* by Laurie Sue Brockway & Victor Fuhrman (Sterling, 2008). We have included it here for you.

Lord God, we bless and praise you for the wonders of your creation, for its rich variety, and its immeasurable abundance.

In your wisdom and love, you created the birds of the air, the fish of the sea, and every living creature and gave to us dominion over them.

They enhance our lives in so many ways and by their very presence give glory to you. They rely on us, as they rely on you, for their well-being.

And so, Father, we ask you to bless (name of animal) here present. May he/she be a living example of your watchful care, and may you grant him/her health, happiness, caring people, and everything needed for the joyous life you intend for him/her.

Praise and glory be to you, Lord God, for ever and ever. Amen

BLESSED OLIVER, HIS DADDY CITO & FATHER PAUL

Directory of Pet Loss Resources

Bibliography

Adamec, Christine. *When Your Pet Dies: Dealing with Your Grief and Helping Your Children Cope.* New York: The Berkley Publishing Group, 1996. *Out of print. Limited availability.*

Anderson, Davis C. *Guide to Pet Loss Resources.* 3rd ed. Victoria, British Columbia: Trafford, 2005.

Anderson, Moira. *Coping with Sorrow on the Loss of Your Pet.* 2nd ed. Loveland, Colo.: Alpine Publications Inc., 1996. *Out of print. Limited availability.*

Antinori, Deborah. *Journey Through Pet Loss.* Audio cassette. Basking Ridge, N.J.: Yoko Spirit Publications, 2000.

Barton Ross, Cheri. *Pet Loss and Children: Establishing a Healthy Foundation.* New York: Brunner-Routledge, 2005.

Barton Ross, Cheri, et al. *Pet Loss and Human Emotion: A Guide to Recovery.* 2nd ed. New York: Brunner-Routledge, 2007.

Becker, Marty. *The Healing Power of Pets: Harnessing the Ability of Pets to Make and Keep People Happy and Healthy.* New York: Hyperion, 2002.

Brackenridge, Sandra S. *Because of Flowers and Dancers.* Santa Barbara, Calif.: Veterinary Practice Publishing Co.,1994. *Out of print. Not available.*

Bronson, Howard. *Dog Gone: Coping with the Loss of a Pet.* Rev. ed. Sandwich, Mass.: Bestsell Publications, 2000.

Brown, Robin Jean. *How to Roar: Pet Loss Grief Recovery.* Morrisville, N.C.: Lulu Press, 2005.

Buddemeyer-Porter, Mary. *Will I See Fido in Heaven?: Scripturally Revealing God's Eternal Plan for His Lesser Creatures.* Manchester, Mo.: Eden Publications, 1995.

Canfield, Jack, ed., et al. *Chicken Soup for the Pet Lover's Soul.* Deerfield Beach, Fla.: Health Communications, 1998.

Carmack, Betty J. *Grieving the Death of a Pet.* Minneapolis, Minn.: Augsburg Fortress Press, 2003.

Church, Julie Adams and Constance Coleman. *Joy in a Woolly Coat: Living with, Loving, and Letting Go of Treasured Animal Friends.* Tiburon, Calif.: H.J. Kramer, 1988.

Coleman, Joan. *Forever Friends: Resolving Grief After the Loss of a Beloved Animal.* Las Vegas, Nev.: J.C. Tara Enterprises, Inc., 1993.

Colgrove, Melba, et al. *How to Survive the Loss of a Love.* 2nd ed. Los Angeles: Prelude Press, 1991.

Congalton, David. *Three Cats, Two Dogs: One Journey Through Multiple Pet Loss.* Troutdale, Ore.: NewSage Press, 2000.

Davis, Christine. *For Every Cat an Angel.* Portland, Ore.: Lighthearted Press, 2001.

Davis, Christine. *For Every Dog an Angel.* Portland, Ore.: Lighthearted Press, 2001.

Deits, Bob. *Life after Loss.* 2nd ed. Tucson, Ariz.: Fisher Books, 1992. *Out of print. Limited availability.*

Fujimoto Nakaya, Shannon. *Kindred Spirit, Kindred Care: Making Health Decisions on Behalf of Our Animal Companions.* Novato, Calif.: New World Library, 2005.

Gilbert, Laynee. *I Remember You: A Grief Journal.* San Jose, Calif.: L.O.A. Publications, 2000.

Gilbert, Laynee. *Precious Companion: A Book of Comfort and Remembrance After the Loss of a Pet.* San Jose, Calif.: L.O.A. Publications, 2007.

Greene, Lorri and Jacquelyn Landis. *Saying Good-Bye to the Pet You Love: A Complete Resource to Help You Heal.* Oakland, Calif.: New Harbinger Publications, 2002.

Gustafson, Mickie. *Losing Your Dog: Coping with Grief When Your Pet Dies.* New York: Bergh Publishing, 1991.

Harris, Eleanor. *Pet Loss: A Spiritual Guide.* St. Paul, Minn.: Llewellyn Publications, 1997.

Harris, Julia A. *Pet Loss: A Spiritual Guide.* New York: Lantern Books, 2002.

Haymes, Peggy and Lautemann, Susan. *Grieving the Loss of Your Pet.* Audio CD. Winston-Salem, N.C.: Kalalogos, 2003.

Hill, Sarah Ann. *Ophelia's Winter.* Bloomington, Ind.: First Books, 2000.

Hunt, Laurel E. *Angel Pawprints.* Pasadena, Calif.: Darrowby Press, 1998. *Out of print. Limited availability.*

Hunt, Laurel E., *Angel Whiskers.* New York: Hyperion, 2000. *Out of print. Limited availability.*

Ironside, Virginia. *Good-Bye, Dear Friend: Coming to Terms with the Death of a Pet.* London: Robson Books, 1994.

James, John. *The Grief Recovery Handbook.* New York: Harper Collins, 1988. *Out of print. Limited availability.*

James, John W. and Russell Friedman. *When Children Grieve: For Adults to Help Children Deal with Death, Divorce, Pet Loss, Moving and Other Losses.* London: Perennial, 2002.

Johns, Bud, ed. *Old Dogs Remembered.* San Francisco: Synergistic Press, Inc., 1999.

Kaufman, Julie, D.C., C.A.C. *Crossing the Rubicon: Celebrating the Human-Animal Bond in Life and Death.* Cottage Grove, Wisc.: Xenophon Publications, 1999.

Kay, William J., et al. *Pet Loss and Human Bereavement.* Ames, Iowa: Blackwell Professional, 1995.

Kelleher, Susan and Rod Lawrence. *Spirit Dogs: Heroes in Heaven.* Silverthrone, Colo.: Owl of Athene Press, 1998.

Knapp, Caroline. *Pack of Two: The Intricate Bond between People and Dogs.* New York: Broadway Books, 1999.

Kosins, Martin. *Maya's First Rose: Diary of a Very Special Love.* Royal Oaks, Mich.: Open Sky Books, 1992.

Kowalski, Gary. *Good-bye, Friend.* Walpole, N. H.: Stillpoint Publishing International, 1997.

Kurz, Gary. *Cold Noses At the Pearly Gates: A Book of Hope.* Friendswood, Tex.: Cold Noses, 1997.

Lagoni, Laurel, Carolyn Butler, and Suzanne Hetts. *The Human-Animal Bond and Grief.* Philadelphia: W.B. Saunders, 1994.

Lee, L. and M. Bucks. *Absent Friend.* High Wycombe, Bucks, United Kingdom: Henston, Ltd., 1992. *Out of print. Limited availability.*

Lemieux, Christina M. *Coping with the Loss of a Pet: A Gentle Guide for All Who Love a Pet.* Reading, Pa.: Wallace R. Clark Publishers, 1988.

Luckenbach, Patty L. *The Kingdom of Heart: A Pet Loss Journal.* Burbank, Calif.: Spiritual Living Press, 2005.

Matschek, Cheryl A. *For the Love of Princess: Surviving the Loss of Your Pet.* Albuquerque, N.M.: Princess Pub., 1998.

McClinton, James L., PhD *Paw Prints in Heaven? Christians and Pet Loss.* Lincoln, Neb.: iUniverse, Inc., 2004.

Milani, Myrna M. *Preparing for the Loss of Your Pet: Saying Good-bye with Love, Dignity, and Peace of Mind.* Rocklin, Calif.: Prima Publishing, 1998. *Out of print. Limited availability.*

Montgomery, M. and H. Montgomery. *Good-bye My Friend.* Minneapolis, Minn.: Montgomery Press, 1991.

Mooney, Samantha. *A Snowflake in My Hand.* New York: Delacorte, 1983.

Nieberg, Herbert, Ph.D. *Pet Loss: A Thoughtful Guide for Adults and Children.* New York: Harper & Row, 1982, 1996.

Nieberg, Kay, et al. *Pet Loss and Human Bereavement: A Symposium.* Ames, Iowa: Iowa State University Press, 1984.

Nolfo-Wheeler, Amy and N. A. Noel. *All God's Creatures Go to Heaven.* Indianapolis, Ind.: Noel Studio, 1996.

Olson, Marsha. *Dogwood and Catnip: Living Tributes to Pets We Have Loved and Lost.* Minneapolis, Minn.: Fairview Press, 2003.

O'Neill, Eugene. *The Last Will and Testament of an Extremely Distinguished Dog.* Reprint. New York: Henry Holt & Company, Inc., 1999.

Pasick, Robert S. *Conversations with My Old Dog: For Anyone Who Has Ever Loved and Lost a Pet.* Chicago: Transitions Bookplace, 2000.

Peterson, Linda, ed. *Surviving the Heartbreak of Choosing Death for Your Pet.* West Chester, Pa.: Greentree Publishing, 1997.

Pomerance, Diane. *When Your Pet Dies.* Bartonville, Tex.: Polaire Publications, 2001.

Potter, J., Jr. and George Koss. *Death of a Pet: Answers to Questions for Children and Animal Lovers of All Ages.* Stamford, N.Y.: Guideline Publications, 1991.

Quackenbush, Jamie and Denise Graveline. *When Your Pet Dies: How to Cope with Your Feelings.* New York: Simon & Schuster, 1985.

Quintana, Maria L., et al. *It's Okay To Cry.* Rev. ed. Perrysburg, Ohio: Mariposa Press, 2000.

Reynolds, Rita M. *Blessing the Bridge: What Animals Teach Us About Death, Dying, and Beyond.* Troutdale, Ore: NewSage Press, 2000.

Sife, Wallace, Ph.D. *The Loss of a Pet: A Guide to Coping with the Grieving Process When a Pet Dies.* 3rd ed. New York: Howell Book House, 2005.

Smith, Kymberly. *Healing the Pain of Pet Loss: Letters in Memoriam.* Philadelphia: Charles Press Publisher, 1997.

Smith, Scott S. *The Soul of Your Pet: Evidence for the Survival of Animals in the Afterlife.* Sequim, Wash.: Holmes Publishing Group, 1998.

Stern, Michael and Susan Cropper. *Loving and Losing a Pet: A Psychologist and a Veterinarian Share Their Wisdom.* Northvale, N.J.: Jason Aronson Inc., 1998.

Stuparyk, Emily. *When Only the Love Remains: The Pain of Pet Loss.* Winnipeg, Canada: Stuparyk Publishing, 1998.

Tousley, Marty and Katherine Heuerman. *The Final Farewell: Preparing For and Mourning the Loss of Your Pet.* Phoenix, Ariz.: Our Pals Publishing Co., 1997. *Out of print. Limited availability.*

Townsend, Irving. *Separate Lifetimes.* Exeter, N.H.: Townsend Publishing, 1986.

Traisman, Enid. *My Personal Pet Remembrance Journal.* Wenatchee, Wash.: Direct Book Service, 1995.

Underhill, Cheryl, M. Ed., LPC. *Geadon's Gift: Surviving the Loss of Your Pet.* Geadon's Gift Publications, 1997.

Wagner, Teresa L. and Maxine Musgrave, illustrator. *Legacies of Love: A Gentle Guide to Healing from the Loss of Your Animal Loved One.* Audio cassette. Matters of the Heart, 1998.

Walker, Kaetheryn. *The Heart That Is Loved Never Forgets.* Rochester, Vt.: Healing Arts Press, 1999.

Watson, George and Emily Watson. *Dogs Have Souls Too: The Spirit of Miss Sarah.* Salt Lake City, Utah: PMD Publishing, 2000.

Weaver, Helen. *The Daisy Sutra.* Woodstock, N.Y.: Buddha Rock Press, 2001.

Webb, Cheryl Reneé. *Do Pets and Other Animals Go to Heaven? How to Recover From the Loss of an Animal Friend.* Ortonville, Mich.: BriteBooks, 2002.

Wood, Barbara, et al. *Pet Loss Symposiums: Delta Society Conference Lecture Summaries and Writings on Pet Owners' Grief, Bereavement Therapy, and Human Nature.* Bellevue, Wash.: Delta Society, 1999.

Books for Children

*"There is only one smartest dog in the world and
every child has it."*

Beckmann, Roberta. *Children Who Grieve: A Manual for Conducting Support Groups*. Holmes Beach, Fla.: Learning Publications, Inc., 1990. *Out of print. Limited availability.*

Blain Parker, Marjorie. *Jasper's Day*. Toronto/New York: Kids Can Press, 2002.

Brady, Irene. *Mouse Named Mus*. Boston: Houghton-Mifflin, 1972.

Buscaglia, Leo. *The Fall of Freddie the Leaf: 20th Anniversary Edition*. New York: Holt, Rinehart & Winston, 2002.

Cardeccia, Kimberly A. *Healing Your Heart When Your Animal Friend is Gone: A Children's Pet Bereavement Workbook*. Howell, Mich.: Bree's Gift Publishing, 2004.

Carrick, C. *The Accident.* New York: Clarion Books, 1976.

Dalpra-Berman, Gina. *Remembering Pets.* San Francisco: Robert Reed Publishers, 2001.

Graeber, Charlotte. *Mustard.* New York: Macmillan, 1988.

Greenberg, Judith E. and Carey, Helen H. *Sunny: The Death of a Pet.* New York: Franklin Watts, 1986.

Grollman, Earl. *Bereaved Children and Teens: A Support Guide for Parents and Professionals.* Boston: Beacon Press, 1995.

Grollman, Earl. *Talking about Death: A Dialog between Parent and Child.* Boston: Beacon Press, 1990.

Harris, Robie H. and Jan Ormerod, illustrator. *Good-bye Mousie.* New York: Margaret K. McElderry, 2001.

Hewett, Joan. *Rosalie.* New York: William Morrow & Co., 1987.

Hurd, Edith Thatcher. *The Black Dog Who Went Into the Woods.* New York: Harper & Row, 1980.

Johnston, Marianne. *Let's Talk About When Your Pet Dies.* New York: The Let's Talk Library, 1998.

Leaf, Munro. *Noodle.* New York: Scholastic Book Services, 1971.

Makkay, Linda and Marlene Hingstman, illustrator. *When Kitty Passed Away: Explaining Pet Cremation to a Child.* Edina, Minn.: Beaver's Pond Press, 2007.

Mellonie, Brian and Robert Ingpen. *Lifetimes: The Beautiful Way to Explain Death to Children.* New York: Bantam Books, Inc., 1983.

Moorhead, Debby. *A Special Place for Charles: A Child's Companion Through Pet Loss.* Broomfield, Colo.: Partners in Publishing, 1996.

Napoli, Donna Jo. *The Bravest Thing*. New York: Dutton Children's Books, 1995.

Patterson, Dr. Francine. *Koko's Kitten*. Reading Rainbow Book. New York: Scholastic, Inc., 1985. *Out of print. Limited availability.*

Rogers, Fred. *When a Pet Dies*. First Experiences Series. New York: Putnam Publishing Group, 1998.

Sanford, Doris. *It Must Hurt a Lot*. Portland, Ore.: Multnomah Press, 1986, 1997. *Out of print. Limited availability.*

Simon, Norma. *The Saddest Time*. Morton Grove, Ill.: Albert Whitman & Company, 1986.

Stolz, Mary. *King Emmett the Second*. New York: Greenwillow Books, 1991.

Tester, Sylvia Root. *Sad (What Does It Mean?)*. Elgin, Ill.: The Child's World, 1980.

Thomas, Jane Resh. *The Comeback Dog*. New York: Bantam-Skylark, 1984.

Thompson, Eileen. *The Golden Coyote*. New York: Simon & Schuster Children's Book Div., 1971.

Tobias, Tobi. *Petey*. New York: G. P. Putnam's Sons, 1978.

Tousley, Marty. *Children and Pet Loss: A Guide for Helping*. Scottsdale, Ariz.: Companion Animal Association of Arizona, 1996.

VanderWyden, William. *Butterflies: Talking with Children about Death and Life Eternal*. New York: Tabor, 1991. *Out of print. Limited availability.*

Viorst, Judith. *The Tenth Good Thing About Barney.* New York: Atheneum, 1971.

Warburg, Sandol. *Growing Time.* Boston: Houghton-Mifflin, 1969.

Wilhelm, Hans. *I'll Always Love You.* New York: Crown Publishers, 1985.

White, E. B. *Charlotte's Web.* New York: Dell Publishing Co., 1952.

Special Recommendations

Brockway, Laurie Sue & Victor Fuhrman. *Pet Prayers & Blessings: Ceremonies & Celebrations to Share With the Animals You Love.* New York: Sterling Publishing Co., Inc., 2008.

Cotner, June. *Dog Blessings: Poems, Prose, and Prayers Celebrating Our Relationship with Dogs.* Novato, Calif.: New World Library, 2008.

Cotner, June. *Animal Blessings: Prayers and Poems Celebrating Our Pets.* San Francisco: HarperCollins, 2000.

Myron, Vicki with Bret Witter. *Dewey: The Small-Town Library Cat Who Touched the World.* New York: Grand Central Publishing, Hachette Book Group, 2008.

Support Hotlines:
Pet Loss and Bereavement Services

- **The American Society for the Prevention of Cruelty to Animals (ASPCA) National Pet Loss Hotline**

  o   424 East 92 Street, New York, NY 10128

  o   Phone: 212-876-7700, extension 4355

  o   Fax: 212-860-3435

  o   E-mail: StephanieL@ASPCA.org

  o   Contact: Stephanie LaFarge, Ph.D.

The ASPCA Counseling Department offers a full range of pet loss and bereavement services. The National Pet Loss Hotline offers free nationwide consultation to bereaved owners on a twenty-four-hour basis. Call 1-800-946-4646, use keypad to punch in pin number 140-7211, and then your own phone number. The call will be returned immediately. New York City residents may be seen in person at the ASPCA headquarters.

- **C.A.R.E. Helpline for Companion Animal Related Emotions**

  o University of Illinois Veterinary Teaching Hospital, 1008 W. Hazelwood Drive, Urbana, IL 61802

  o Phone: Toll free 1-877-394-2273 or local 217-244-2273

  o E-mail: griefhelp@cvm.uiuc.edu

  o Contact: Cheryl Weber cweber79@uiuc.edu

  o Web site: www.cvm.uiuc.edu/CARE

  The death, loss, or impending death of your companion animal can be a difficult and emotional time. The C.A.R.E. Helpline was developed to provide a supportive outlet for people experiencing the loss of a companion animal. Trained veterinary students staff the helpline. You may call and leave a voice mail message at any time. Volunteers will return calls on Tuesday, Thursday, and Sunday between 7–9 PM Central Standard Time.

- **The Chicago Veterinary Medical Association Pet Loss Support Helpline**

  o Phone: 630-325-1600

  The Helpline was established in 1993 and provides referral information on professional grief counseling and information packets on children and grief, euthanasia, pet loss and the elderly, and a pet loss bibliography. You may call and leave a voice mail message at any time. A volunteer will pick up messages and call back between 7–9 PM Central Standard Time each weekday evening. There is no charge for this service but long distance calls will be returned collect.

- **CONTACT of Burlington County, NJ (twenty-four-hour crisis helpline)**
  - P.O. Box 131, Moorestown, NJ 08057-0131
  - Phone: 1-800-404-PETS (available only in NJ)
  - Phone: 1-856-234-4688 (outside NJ)

  PetFriends, a free service of CONTACT, provides telephone support, information, and referrals to anyone who is mourning or anticipating the loss of a pet. A licensed clinical social worker and a veterinarian train volunteers.

- **The Iams Pet Loss Support Center and Hotline**
  - Phone: 888-332-7738

  Hours: Monday–Friday, 8 AM –5 PM

- **The Ohio State University Companion Animal Listening Line**
  - Phone : 614-292-1823

  Hours: Monday–Friday, 6:30–9:30 PM;
  Saturday–Sunday 10 AM –4 PM Eastern Standard Time
  Most hotline volunteers are veterinary students, therefore, hours are dependent on volunteer availability and may be more limited during summer months.

- **P.A.T.S. (Pet Loss Support Line)**

  o Pacific Animal Therapy Society, 9412 Laurie's Lane, Sidney, B.C., V8L 4L2, Canada

  o Phone: 250-389-8047

Call between 8 AM –9 PM any day of the week and leave your name and number. All long distance calls are returned collect.

- **Pet Grief Support Service**

  o Companion Animal Association of Arizona Inc., P.O. Box 5006, Scottsdale, AZ 85261-5006

  o Pet Grief Support Helpline Phone: 602-995-5885

  o Association Phone: 602-258-3306

Whether you are anticipating or coping with the loss of a beloved companion animal, the Pet Grief Support Service recognizes your pain and offers you understanding, compassion, and support. Operated entirely by trained volunteers who themselves have suffered the loss of a pet, the service provides an informational telephone helpline directing callers to monthly pet loss support group meetings, pet grief information, literature and reading lists, and referrals to appropriate resources. Although unable to take messages or return calls to the helpline at this time, they can help point you to other available pet loss resources.

- **Pet Loss Support Hotline**

  o Center for Animals in Society, School of Veterinary Medicine, University of California, Davis, CA 95616

  o Phone: 1-800-565-1526

  o Contact: Bonnie S. Mader, M.S., Associate Director/ Hotline Coordinator

  Hours: Monday–Friday 6:30–9:30 PM Pacific Standard Time

- **Pet Loss Support Hotline**

  o Companion Animal Hospital, Box 35, College of Veterinary Medicine, Cornell University, Ithaca, NY 14853-6401

  o Phone: 607-253-3932

  o Web site: www.vet.cornell.edu/public/petloss/

  Hours: Tuesday-Thursday, 6-9 PM Eastern Standard Time

- **The Pet Loss Support Hotline**

  o Iowa State University. 2116 College of Veterinary Medicine, Ames, IA 50011

  o Phone: 1-888-478-7574

  o Web site: www.vetmed.iastate.edu/animals/petloss/ default.html

  Hours: September–April, seven days a week 6–9 PM;

May–August, Monday, Wednesday, and Friday 6–9 PM Central Standard Time

- **Pet Loss Support Hotline**

  o Tufts University, Boston, MA

  o Phone: 508-839-7966

  o Web site: www.tufts.edu/vet/petloss/

  Hours: Monday–Friday, 6–9 PM Eastern Standard Time

- **Pet Loss Support Hotline**

  o University of Florida, College of Veterinary Medicine, Gainesville, FL

  o Phone: 352-392-4700, extension 4080

  Call at any time and leave your name and number. You will be called back between the hours of 7–9 PM Eastern Standard Time. The University of Florida offers telephone support anywhere in the United States at no charge.

- **Pet Loss Support Hotline**

  o Virginia-Maryland Regional College of Veterinary Medicine

  o Phone: 540-231-8038

  Hours: Tuesday and Thursday, 6–9 PM Eastern Standard Time

- **Pet Loss Support Hotline**

  o Washington State University, College of Veterinary Medicine, Pullman, WA

  o Phone: 509-335-5704

  Trained WSU veterinary student volunteers staff the phones as compassionate listeners Monday–Thursday from 6:30–9 PM and Saturday 1–3 PM Pacific Standard Time. Calls received after hours will be promptly returned on a collect basis.

- **Pet Loss Support Program**

  o Michigan State University College of Veterinary Medicine, G-145 Veterinary Medical Center, East Lansing, MI 48824-1314

  o Web site: www.cvm.msu.edu/petloss/index.htm

  o Pet Loss Support Hotline: 517-432-2696

  Staffed by volunteer veterinary students who receive training in grief support, the hotline operates Tuesday, Wednesday, and Thursday from 6:30–9:30 PM Eastern Standard Time. The pet loss support group meets under the direction of a certified grief counselor. Meetings are held the first Tuesday of each month at 7 PM in the Veterinary Medical Center in East Lansing, MI.

Selected Web Sites

Association for Pet Loss and Bereavement
www.aplb.org

Compilation of Pet Bereavement Centers/Individuals
www.paws-to-heaven.com

Pet Bereavement Counselling (Great Britain)
www.petbereavementcounselling.com

Pet Bereavement Resources
www.catanddog.com

Pet Loss Grief Support
www.petloss.com

Disclaimer

The purpose of the directory of pet loss resources is to inform you about resources available. We do not endorse or recommend any of the individuals or organizations listed herein. We have no control over the services provided and have no mechanism for judging or verifying the competence of the individuals or organizations listed herein. Every effort was made to ensure that the information herein was accurate at the time of publication; we assume no responsibility for any changes made by individuals or businesses.

Special Announcement: The Perseus Foundation is pleased to announce our chat room will be opened in fall 2009. We are currently looking for warmhearted, compassionate volunteers who are able to listen, comfort, and provide gentle solace to those who have just lost a beloved animal companion. Father Paul's book will be our teaching guide. www.perseusfoundation.org

River of Hearts

We are deeply indebted to Father Paul's friends,
especially those at his parish,
Our Lady of Peace Church,
Manhattan, New York, and
Hartsdale Pet Cemetery, The Peaceable Kingdom,
Hartsdale, New York,
for their kindness in making this book a reality
with their generous donations.

Our *River of Hearts* in memory of these beloved pets:

Mishka Martin	Katy Martin
Sedona Martin	Sasha Martin

Freckles Martin

Foxy Clipper

Gourmet Muffin McConnell   Ray + Elaine's Vesti

Vinca   Prince Teddy Hoffman

Max Molinari   Zackary Schermerhorn

Blackie Boccanfuso   Lucas Schermerhorn

PUSILLIA & "AUNT" HORTY, 1933

Kelly Ann Caruso

Priscilla Caruso

Willow Caruso

Prince Caruso

Cassie Browne

Dirigo Browne

Happy

Rusty Caruso

Tippy Caruso

Tootsie Onorato

Toto Fekert

Torito Gulick

DUCHESS, 1938

Cyrus Biggington Moorman

Sophie Moorman

Cleo Moorman

Rosie Teresse Moorman

Princess Annalena Catisina Moorman
(cat named Annie who crowned herself)

Petunia

Nickie Brady

Smokey Pilbat

Shepard of Bellehaven
("Shep") Travers Yostpille

SUGAR, 1950s

Figaro Guatelli	Alcott Smith
Rocky Dooner	Zoe
Pixie Dooner	Tip D'Arcy
	Oliver Lachman
Pinky Dvorak	
Chicky Dvorak	Max Flynn
Happy Dvorak	Lady Puff Flynn
Skinny Dvorak	Boots Ellis
	Muffin Ellis
Missy Gavin	
Tiger Dvorak	Bugsy McGuinness
Lucky Dvorak	Silver Peterson

Dandelion Dodge	Trey
Fridge Dodge	Pusillia
Huntress Butler	Bruno
Rhett Butler	Lord Cholmondeley
Scarlett O'Hara Butler	Angel Ruta
Ashley Butler	Sugar Zappo
Mr. Boo Butler	Candy Zappo
Poochie	Charlie Browne Zappo
Dante Tort	Jaspur Zappo
Duchess	Angelique Pippin Zappo

CANDY, 1960s

River of Stars

Our *River of Stars* in honor of these living paws:

Faye Martin   Cary Martin

Cora Bear Charlton
(Father Paul taught her to pray before lunch)

CORA BEAR

Oliver Orlick Estevez

Ralph Mariani

Emily Caruso

Kasa Detrow

Hunter Ronan

Bailey Fekert

Barkley Koss

Rodrigo Gomez

Jasmine Alarcon

Lucy Molinari

Josephine Boccanfuso

Lucy Boccanfuso

Bella Alleluia

Frodo Alleluia

THADDEUS SELVAGGIO

Hannah Schermerhorn

Priscilla Pussycat Pilbat Travers

Phoenix Moorman

House Wolfie Moorman

Merster Moorman
(the Clint Eastwood of cats)

Drifter

Jamie Brady

Star Dooner

Plum Lynch

Mickey Lynch

MASSI GERARDI

Alanna Doyle

Maggie Ellis

Charlie Ellis

Flash

Zoe Dodge

Tigger Dodge

Miss Pepper Dodge

Clarence Butler

Sally Lowenthal

Stella

Hailey

Lucy Dodge

Max Ruta

Houdini Mishu Zappo

LULU & STELLA, 2008

FLAKE, 2009

Printed in the United States
By Bookmasters